The Art of Habit Mastery

Unleashing Your Full Potential for Personal Growth

ANIL K. ARORA

Made with ❤ on the Notion Press Platform

www.notionpress.com

To my dear parents,

I dedicate these words to you, the ones who have always supported and encouraged me in everything I do. You have been my constant source of inspiration, motivation, and strength. Your love and guidance have helped me become the person I am today.

This book is a reflection of the values and lessons you have instilled in me throughout my life. Your unwavering belief in me has given me the confidence to pursue my dreams, and I am forever grateful.

I hope this book serves as a testament to your unwavering love and support. Thank you for being my guiding light and for always believing in me.

With love and gratitude,

Anil K Arora

Contents

Foreword

We all have habits, both good and bad, that shape our lives in profound ways. Our habits can either help us achieve our goals and aspirations or hinder our progress and keep us stuck in a cycle of unproductive behaviors. This is why learning the art of habit mastery is crucial to living a fulfilling and successful life.

In this book, you will learn practical strategies and techniques to help you develop good habits, break bad habits, and sustain the changes you make. From understanding how habits work and why they matter, to developing mental resilience and mindfulness, this book covers everything you need to know to transform your life through the power of habit.

The author's approach is grounded in scientific research and enriched with real-life examples and stories that make this book engaging and relatable. The practical tips and exercises provided in each chapter will help you apply the concepts to your own life and create lasting change.

Whether you want to improve your health, productivity, relationships, or any other area of your life, the principles outlined in this book will help you achieve your goals and become the best version of yourself.

I am honored to have the opportunity to introduce you to this remarkable book and the author's wisdom. I am confident that by reading "The Art of Habit Mastery," you will gain valuable insights and tools to help you transform your life and master the art of habit formation.

Anil K Arora

Preface

Habits are the building blocks of our lives, shaping our behavior and determining our outcomes. We all have habits, both good and bad, that have a profound impact on our success, health, relationships, and happiness. Despite their importance, many of us struggle to create lasting change and develop good habits.

This book is for anyone who wants to understand the science of habit formation and learn practical strategies to master their habits. Whether you want to break bad habits, develop good habits, or sustain the changes you make, this book will provide you with the tools and insights you need to transform your life.

Drawing on the latest research in psychology, neuroscience, and behavioral science, this book offers a comprehensive framework for understanding how habits work and why they matter. You will learn how to identify your current habits, set effective goals, develop mental resilience, cultivate mindfulness, and build a supportive environment that empowers you to succeed.

Each chapter is designed to be actionable and engaging, with real-life examples and stories to illustrate the concepts and techniques. You will find practical tips, exercises, and tools to help you apply the principles to your own life and make lasting change.

I wrote this book with the hope of inspiring and empowering readers to take control of their habits and create the life they deserve. I believe that with the right mindset, strategies, and support, anyone can master their habits and achieve their goals.

Thank you for joining me on this journey of self-discovery and transformation. I hope that this book will help you unlock your full potential and become the best version of yourself.

Anil K Arora

Acknowledgments

Writing this book has been a journey of self-discovery and growth, and I am grateful for the many people who have supported me along the way.

First and foremost, I want to thank God for giving me the strength, inspiration, and guidance to pursue this project. Without His blessings, I could not have accomplished this feat.

I am deeply indebted to my parents, whose love, encouragement, and sacrifices have made me who I am today. Their unwavering faith in me has been a constant source of motivation and inspiration.

My brother Happie has been my rock throughout this process, always there to listen, support, and encourage me. His insights and feedback have been invaluable, and I am grateful for his unwavering support.

I want to express my heartfelt gratitude to my dearest friend Shreya Kashyap, whose friendship and support have been a constant source of joy and inspiration. Her kindness, intelligence, and unwavering support have helped me navigate the ups and downs of the writing process.

I also want to thank all the friends, colleagues, and mentors who have provided me with feedback, support, and encouragement throughout this journey. Your insights, suggestions, and encouragement have been invaluable, and I am grateful for your support.

Finally, I want to thank the readers of this book, whose interest, feedback, and support have inspired me to share my knowledge and insights. I hope that this book will help you master your habits and achieve your goals.

Thank you all from the bottom of my heart.

Anil K Arora

Hey Dear,

Thank you so much for your unwavering support. Your encouragement has meant the world to me. I hope this book brings you as much joy as writing it brought me.

Warmly.

Anil K Arora

Prologue/Introduction

Habits are an integral part of our lives. We all have habits that we want to cultivate, and others that we want to get rid of. Whether it's waking up early, exercising regularly, or quitting smoking, changing our habits is one of the most challenging and rewarding things we can do.

As someone who has struggled with developing good habits and breaking bad ones, I understand the difficulties and frustrations that come with the process. But over time, I have come to appreciate the power of habits in shaping our lives and achieving our goals.

In this book, I want to share what I have learned about habit formation, and provide practical tips and strategies for mastering your habits. Drawing on the latest research in psychology, neuroscience, and behavior change, I will provide insights into how habits work and why they matter, and offer strategies for identifying your current habits, breaking bad habits, and developing good ones.

Through personal stories, examples, and case studies, I will illustrate how habits can impact our lives, and show how changing our habits can lead to profound personal transformation. I will also explore the importance of goal setting, accountability, and social support in habit formation, and provide practical tips for staying on track and avoiding relapse.

My hope is that this book will inspire and empower you to master your habits, and achieve your personal and professional goals. Whether you are looking to become more productive, healthier, or happier, this book will provide you with the tools and insights you need to succeed.

So let's begin this journey together, and discover the art of habit mastery.

Chapter 1: Understanding Habits: How They Work and Why They Matter

Prashant sits at his desk, surrounded by stacks of paperwork and a never-ending to-do list. As a bank manager at Punjab National Bank, he's used to the long hours and high-pressure environment, but lately, it's been taking a toll on him.

He rubs his eyes, feeling the strain of staring at a computer screen for hours on end. He knows he should take a break, but he can't seem to tear himself away from his work. There's always more to do, more clients to serve, more problems to solve.

When he finally does leave the office, he's too wired to relax. He tries to read a book, but his mind keeps drifting back to work. He tries to watch TV, but he can't seem to focus on the plot. He checks his phone, scrolling through social media and emails, but it only makes him more anxious.

As the night wears on, Prashant feels more and more restless. He knows he should be sleeping, but his mind is racing with all the things he has to do tomorrow. He tries to shut off his thoughts, but they keep coming back, like a never-ending loop.

Eventually, he falls asleep, but it's fitful and restless. When he wakes up in the morning, he feels like he hasn't slept at all. He drags himself out of bed and starts his day, but he's already exhausted.

As the days go by, Prashant's lack of sleep starts to affect every aspect of his life. He's irritable with his coworkers, short-tempered with his family, and too tired to exercise or pursue his hobbies. He knows he needs to make a change, but he doesn't know where to start.

We all have habits like Prashant's that we want to change. Maybe it's eating too much junk food, or procrastinating on work assignments. But what are habits, exactly? And why are they so hard to break?

As Prashant delves deeper into his research, he realizes that habits are behaviors that are repeated regularly and often unconsciously. They are formed through a process called habituation, where the brain learns to associate a particular action with a particular reward.

He learns that habits are so hard to break because they are deeply ingrained in our neural pathways. They become automatic and hardwired into our brains, making it difficult to consciously override them.

Luckily for Prashant, he meets a mentor, a habit change expert who helps him to understand the science behind habits and how they are formed. The mentor explains to Prashant that habits are actually a product of his brain's efficiency, allowing him to perform routine tasks without having to consciously think about them.

The mentor further explains that habits have three components: the cue, the routine, and the reward. The cue is the trigger that initiates the habit, the routine is the behavior itself, and the reward is the positive reinforcement that reinforces the habit.

With his mentor's help, Prashant starts to identify the cues and rewards that are driving his own habit of staying up late and scrolling through social media. He realizes that the cue is often feeling stressed or overwhelmed at work, and the reward is the temporary distraction and relaxation he gets from scrolling through his phone.

The mentor advises Prashant to experiment with different routines that can give him the same reward without the negative consequences of lost sleep and increased stress. They work together to create a new routine for Prashant, such as taking a short walk or reading a book before bed, which can help him to relax and unwind without the negative effects of social media.

Prashant is amazed at the power of understanding habits and how they can be changed through intentional and conscious effort. He realizes that changing habits is not a matter of willpower alone, but also requires an understanding of the underlying psychological and neurological mechanisms behind them.

What Are Habits?

Habits are automatic behaviors that we repeat without thinking. They're actions that we do on a regular basis, often in response to a specific trigger or cue. For example, Prashant's habit of scrolling through social media late at night might be triggered by feeling bored or anxious.

Habits can be both good and bad. Managing his finances wisely and prudently is a good habit that helps keep his finances healthy. But smoking cigarettes is a bad habit that can lead to serious health problems.

The Power of Habits

Habits are incredibly powerful. They're the building blocks of our daily lives. In fact, studies have shown that as much as 40% of our daily actions are based on habits rather than conscious decisions.

Why do habits have such a strong hold on us? It's because they're efficient. Habits allow our brains to conserve energy and focus on more important tasks. When we perform a habit, our brains go into autopilot mode, conserving mental resources.

But habits aren't just efficient; they're also powerful. Once a habit is formed, it's hard to break. This is because habits become ingrained in our brains over time. They create neural pathways that become stronger every time we repeat the behavior.

How Habits Are Formed

Habits are formed through a process called "habituation." This is when a behavior becomes automatic after repeated exposure to a specific stimulus or trigger. For example, if Prashant hears his phone beep, he might automatically reach for it without thinking.

Habit formation has three main components: the cue, the routine, and the reward. The cue is the trigger that prompts the behavior. The routine is the behavior itself. And the reward is the positive outcome that reinforces the behavior.

Here are the three components of habits:

- **The Cue:**

  The cue is the trigger or signal that initiates a habit. It is the event, situation, or context that automatically prompts us to engage in a particular behavior. The cue can be any sensory or environmental factor that is linked with the habit. For example, the sound of an alarm can be a cue for waking up in the morning.

- **The Routine:**

  The routine is the actual behavior or action that is performed in response to the cue. It is the habit itself, the automatic response that follows the cue. The routine can be a physical behavior, a thought process, or an emotional response. For example, taking a sip of coffee and celebrating its aroma.

- **The Reward:**

  The reward is the positive outcome that is associated with the habit. It is the benefit or the pleasure that we gain from performing the habit. The reward reinforces the habit and encourages us to repeat it in the future. The reward can be anything that we find satisfying or pleasurable, such as the taste of food, the sense of accomplishment, or the feeling of relaxation. For example, feeling alert and energized after drinking coffee.

The three components of habits - cue, routine, and reward - work together to create an automatic and repetitive behavior. By understanding these components, we can develop an awareness of our habits and how they work, which can help us modify or change our habits to achieve personal growth and positive change.

Habits are important because they have a significant impact on our daily lives, influencing our thoughts, actions, and behaviors. Here are several reasons why habits matter:

Habits are automatic and require less mental effort: Habits are behaviors that we perform automatically without much conscious thought or effort. When we repeat a behavior consistently, our brain learns to recognize the cue and the routine and performs them almost automatically. This saves mental effort and allows us to focus on other tasks or decisions.

Habits shape our daily routines: Habits are an essential part of our daily routines. Our routines determine how we spend our time, which tasks we prioritize, and how we approach our work and personal life. Positive habits can help us manage our time and energy better, reduce stress, and increase our productivity.

Habits influence our decision-making: Our habits can influence the choices we make, even when they are not directly related to the habit. For example, someone who has a habit of going to the gym every morning may be more likely to make healthy food choices throughout the day.

Habits can contribute to personal growth: Positive habits can help us achieve personal growth by promoting positive change in our lives. By developing good habits, such as regular exercise or daily meditation, we can improve our health, reduce stress, and enhance our overall well-being.

Let's look at an example. Prashant has a habit of going to the gym every morning. The cue might be his alarm going off at 6am. The routine is going to the gym and working out. And the reward is the feeling of accomplishment and energy he gets from exercising.

Over time, the cue and reward become associated in his brain, creating a neural pathway. This pathway becomes stronger every time he repeats the behavior, making the habit more automatic and harder to break.

Why Habits Matter

Habits are important because they shape our daily lives. They determine how we spend our time, what we eat, how we interact with others, and much more. If we have good habits, we're more likely to be successful and happy. But if we have bad habits, they can hold us back and lead to negative outcomes.

For example, if Prashant continues his habit of staying up late every night, it could lead to negative consequences such as fatigue, poor work performance, and a weakened immune system. On the other hand, if he develops a good habit of getting enough sleep every night, he'll be more alert, productive, and healthier.

Habits also have a cumulative effect. Small habits, like drinking a glass of water every morning, can add up to big changes over time. Over months or years, small habits can lead to significant improvements in our health, relationships, and overall well-being.

Furthermore, habits can be a powerful tool for personal growth and self-improvement. By identifying and changing our bad habits, we can create new, positive habits that help us achieve our goals and reach our potential.

There are some practical examples of how habits work in our daily lives. For instance:

Brushing your teeth every morning after waking up is a habit that's triggered by the cue of getting out of bed. The routine involves brushing your teeth with toothpaste, while the reward is a fresh and clean feeling in your mouth.

Checking your phone first thing in the morning is also a habit that many people have developed.

The cue might be hearing the alarm or seeing the phone, the routine is scrolling through social media or checking email, and the reward is feeling connected or informed.

Going for a run every day after work can be a habit that's triggered by the cue of leaving your workplace. The routine involves changing into workout clothes, running for a certain distance, and feeling a sense of accomplishment after completing the run.

By understanding how habits work and how they shape our daily lives, we can begin to identify the habits that are helping us and the ones that are holding us back. We can then use this knowledge to make intentional changes that lead to personal growth and a more fulfilling life.

Understanding habits is crucial for personal growth, as habits can either support or hinder our progress towards our goals. By becoming aware of our habits and their underlying mechanisms, we can intentionally modify our behaviours and cultivate positive habits that support our personal growth.

Conclusion

In this chapter, we've explored what habits are, how they're formed, and why they matter. We've seen how habits can be both good and bad, and how they shape our daily lives. We've also looked at how habits are formed through habituation, and how they create neural pathways in our brains.

As we move forward in this book, we'll delve deeper into how to identify and change our habits, both good and bad. We'll explore strategies for developing new, positive habits and breaking old, negative ones. We'll also look at the role of goal setting, accountability, and community in habit formation.

Key Points to Remember:

- Habits are automatic behaviours that are formed through consistent repetition.
- Habits have three components: the cue, the routine, and the reward.
- Habits can be positive or negative, and can be changed with intentional effort.

- Understanding your habits is the first step to changing them and achieving personal growth.
- Habits can be formed and changed through intentional repetition, tracking progress, and rewarding positive behaviours.

Chapter 2: Identifying Your Current Habits: The First Step to Change

As Prashant continues on his journey to change his habits, he realizes that the first step is identifying his current habits. This is a crucial step in the habit change process, as it allows him to gain a better understanding of his behaviors and the patterns that lead to them.

Prashant recognizes the importance of identifying his current habits as the first step towards changing them. He decides to create a habit journal as a tool for self-awareness and reflection. By recording his daily habits and routines, he hopes to gain insights into his behaviors and identify patterns that may be hindering his progress.

Prashant's habit journal includes details about his daily activities, such as what he eats for breakfast, how he commutes to work, and how he spends his free time in the evening. He also notes down the time of day, location, and any other relevant information that may influence his habits.

In addition to recording his habits, Prashant also makes a note of the cues and rewards that are driving his behaviors. He identifies specific triggers that prompt him to engage in certain habits, such as feeling bored or stressed, and notes the rewards he receives from these habits, such as feeling relaxed or entertained.

As Prashant continues to use his habit journal, he begins to notice patterns and connections between his habits and the cues and rewards that drive them. He realizes that many of his habits are automatic responses to specific triggers and that changing these habits will require identifying and modifying the cues and rewards associated with them.

Prashant seeks the guidance of a mentor who helps him to understand the science behind habit formation and the role of cues and rewards in shaping behavior. His mentor encourages him to continue using his habit journal as a tool for self-reflection and advises him to pay close attention to the cues and rewards that drive his habits.

Through his habit journal and the guidance of his mentor, Prashant gains a deeper understanding of his behaviors and begins to develop strategies for changing his habits. He learns that by identifying the cues and rewards associated with his habits, he can modify them to create new, more positive routines.

As Prashant looks through his habit journal, he begins to notice patterns in his behavior. He realizes that he often reaches for sugary snacks when he is feeling stressed at work, and that he tends to spend his evenings watching TV instead of engaging in more productive activities.

The act of journaling also helps Prashant to become more mindful of his behaviors. He starts to pay closer attention to his actions and the triggers that lead to them. This increased awareness allows him to start breaking down his habits into smaller, more manageable parts.

Prashant also starts to use the habit loop framework to analyze his habits. He identifies the cue, routine, and reward for each of his habits, and starts to experiment with changing the routine in order to achieve the same reward.

For example, he realizes that his habit of snacking on sugary foods when he is feeling stressed is driven by a cue of feeling overwhelmed at work, and a reward of the temporary distraction and comfort that comes from eating something sweet. Instead of reaching for a candy bar when he feels stressed, he starts to experiment with other routines, such as taking a short walk or practicing deep breathing exercises.

Prashant also recognizes the importance of self-compassion when it comes to changing habits. He realizes that habits are deeply ingrained in his brain, and that it will take time and effort to change them. He learns to be patient with himself, and to celebrate small successes along the way.

As Prashant becomes more skilled at identifying his habits and breaking them down into smaller parts, he begins to feel more in control of his behavior. He realizes that he has the power to change his habits and create a more fulfilling life for himself.

Identifying your current habits is the first step towards making positive changes in your life. Habits are actions or behaviors that we do repeatedly and often unconsciously. They can have a profound impact on our lives, both positively and negatively. By understanding your current habits, you can identify areas of your life that need improvement and make a plan to change them. In this response, I will explain in detail why identifying your current habits is important and provide practical examples to help you understand the process.

Importance of Identifying Your Current Habits:

Identifying your current habits is important for several reasons. Firstly, it helps you understand the behaviors that are holding you back and preventing you from reaching your goals. Once you have identified these habits, you can work on replacing them with more positive behaviors. Secondly, it allows you to take control of your life by becoming more self-aware. When you are aware of your habits, you can make conscious decisions about how to improve your life. Finally, it enables you to be more intentional with your time and energy. By identifying the habits that are not serving you, you can redirect your efforts towards habits that will help you achieve your goals.

Benefits of Tracking Your Habits:

Tracking your habits on a daily basis can have several benefits. Firstly, it helps you become more self-aware. When you track your habits, you start to notice patterns and behaviors that you might not have been aware of before. This increased self-awareness can help you identify areas of your life that need improvement and make a plan to change them.

Secondly, tracking your habits can help you stay motivated. By keeping track of your progress, you can see the positive changes that you are making in your life. This can provide a sense of accomplishment and help you stay motivated to continue making positive changes.

Finally, tracking your habits can help you stay accountable. When you track your habits, you are more likely to stick to your goals because you are holding yourself accountable. By tracking your habits, you can see when you are falling off track and make adjustments to get back on course.

How to Get Started:

Getting started with tracking your habits is easy. You can start by making a list of the habits that you want to track. These could be things like exercise, reading, meditation, or eating healthy. Once you have identified the habits that you want to track, you can create a daily tracker. This could be a simple spreadsheet or a habit tracking app. The important thing is to find a method that works for you and that you will be able to use consistently.

Tips for Tracking Your Habits:

- **Start Small:** Don't try to track too many habits at once. Start with a few habits and gradually add more as you get comfortable with the process.

- **Be Consistent:** Try to track your habits at the same time every day. This will help you create a routine and make it easier to stick to your goals.

- **Celebrate Your Successes:** When you make progress towards your goals, celebrate your successes. This can help you stay motivated and make it more likely that you will continue to make positive changes.

- **Be Flexible:** It's important to be flexible when tracking your habits. If you miss a day or fall off track, don't beat yourself up about it. Just get back on track the next day.

- **Use Visual Cues:** Use visual cues to help you remember to track your habits. For example, you could set a reminder on your phone or leave your habit tracker in a visible place.

Tracking your habits on a daily basis can be a powerful tool to help you make positive changes in your life. By becoming more self-aware, staying motivated, and holding yourself accountable, you can achieve your goals and create positive habits that will last a lifetime. So, start tracking your habits today and see how it can transform your life.

Identifying your current habits is the first step towards making positive changes in your life. By understanding your habits, you can identify areas of your life that need improvement and make a plan to change them. To identify your habits, start by tracking your behavior and becoming more self-aware. Once you have identified your habits, make a plan to replace negative behaviors with more positive ones. With consistent effort and commitment, you can create new habits that will help you achieve your goals and lives.

Practical Examples:

To help you understand the process of identifying your current habits, let's look at some practical examples:

Example 1: Eating Habits

Let's say that you have a habit of snacking on unhealthy foods throughout the day. You might not even realize that you are doing it because it has become so automatic. To identify this habit, you could start tracking what you eat throughout the day. This could be as simple as writing down what you eat in a journal or using a food tracking app. Once you have identified the habit of snacking on unhealthy foods, you can make a plan to replace it with healthier alternatives. For example, you could plan your meals and snacks in advance, stock your fridge with healthy snacks, or drink more water to help you feel full.

Example 2: Social Media Habits

Let's say that you have a habit of scrolling through social media for hours every day. This habit could be preventing you from being productive or spending time with loved ones. To identify this habit, you could start tracking how much time you spend on social media each day. This could be done by setting a timer on your phone or using an app that tracks your screen time. Once you have identified the habit of spending too much time on social media, you can make a plan to limit your usage. For example, you could set a daily time limit for social media, delete the apps from your phone, or schedule specific times of day to check your accounts.

Example 3: Exercise Habits

Let's say that you have a habit of skipping workouts and not making time for exercise. This habit could be negatively impacting your physical and mental health. To identify this habit, you could start tracking how often you exercise and how you feel after each workout. This could be done by using a fitness tracker or simply writing down your exercise routine in a journal. Once you have identified the habit of skipping workouts, you can make a plan to incorporate exercise into your daily routine. For example, you could schedule workouts in your calendar, find a workout buddy to hold you accountable, or join a fitness class to make it more enjoyable.

Tracking your habits on a daily basis can be an effective tool to help you achieve your goals and make positive changes in your life. Habits are actions that we do repeatedly, and by tracking them, we can identify areas that need improvement and make a plan to change them. In this chapter, we will discuss the benefits of tracking your habits on a daily basis, how to get started, and some tips to help you stay on track.

Key points to remember from the Identification of Habits chapter:

- The first step to changing your habits is to identify them. You can do this by keeping a habit journal, which includes details about your daily activities, cues, and rewards.

- It's important to be honest and specific when identifying your habits. For example, instead of writing "I eat unhealthy food," write "I eat a bag of chips every afternoon."

- Habits are often triggered by cues, which can be anything from a certain time of day to a particular emotion. Identifying your cues can help you understand why you engage in certain habits.

- Rewards are what drive habits, and they can be either positive or negative. For example, the reward for eating a bag of chips every afternoon might be the temporary pleasure of the taste, but the negative consequence of feeling sluggish afterwards.

- The process of identifying your habits requires self-reflection and introspection. It may be helpful to seek the guidance of a mentor or coach to help you through this process.

Chapter 3: The Science of Habit Formation: How to Make New Habits Stick

Prashant had been keeping his habit journal for a few weeks now, and he was starting to notice some patterns. He found that he often snacked on junk food in the late afternoon, when he was feeling bored and restless at work. He also noticed that he tended to stay up late on weekends, even though he knew he should be getting more sleep. But now that he had identified these habits, how could he go about changing them?

Prashant turned to his mentor, who explained the science of habit formation. "Habits are formed through a process called habituation," his mentor explained. "When we repeat a behavior in response to a particular cue, our brain starts to associate that cue with the behavior. Over time, this association becomes stronger, and the behavior becomes automatic."

Prashant was fascinated by this explanation. "So if I want to create a new habit, I need to repeat the behavior in response to a specific cue?" he asked.

"Exactly," his mentor replied. "But it's not enough to simply repeat the behavior. You also need to have a clear reward in mind. Our brains are wired to seek out rewards, so if there's no clear reward associated with the behavior, it's unlikely to become a habit."

Prashant thought about this for a moment. "So if I want to start exercising in the morning, I need to find a cue and a reward that will help me stick to it?"

"Exactly," his mentor confirmed. "The cue could be something as simple as putting your workout clothes out the night before, so you see them first thing in the morning. And the reward could be anything that motivates you, whether it's the feeling of accomplishment after a workout or the promise of a delicious breakfast afterwards."

Prashant was starting to see how he could apply this knowledge to his own habits. He decided to start small by focusing on one new habit: drinking more water throughout the day. He identified a cue - seeing his water bottle on his desk - and a reward - the feeling of hydration and increased energy. He also set a reminder on his phone to refill his water bottle every hour.

At first, Prashant found it difficult to remember to drink water throughout the day. But after a few days of consistently repeating the behavior in response to the cue, it started to become automatic. He even found himself looking forward to the feeling of hydration and energy he got from drinking more water.

Encouraged by his success with the water habit, Prashant decided to apply the same principles to other areas of his life. He started setting specific cues and rewards for his other goals, such as getting more sleep and reducing his late-afternoon snacking.

Over time, Prashant found that he was able to create new habits and break old ones by using the principles of habituation. He realized that the key to making a new habit stick was to have a clear cue and reward, and to repeat the behavior consistently over time.

As Prashant continued on his habit change journey, he also discovered the power of positive self-talk and visualisation. By envisioning himself successfully sticking to his new habits and reinforcing his efforts with positive affirmations, he was able to stay motivated and committed to his goals.

Prashant learned that changing habits is a process that requires patience, persistence, and self-reflection. But by understanding the science of habit formation and applying it to his own life, he was able to make lasting changes that improved his health and well-being.

After learning about the science of habit formation, Prashant realized that changing habits is not an overnight process, but rather a gradual one that requires patience, persistence, and self-reflection. He understood that in order to change a habit, he needed to identify the cue, routine, and reward associated with it. By doing so, he could then modify or replace the routine with a more positive one that still satisfies the same cue and reward.

Prashant also learned that it's important to start small when developing new habits, and to be consistent with his efforts. He recognized that it takes time for a new habit to become automatic, and that setbacks and relapses are a normal part of the process. By staying committed and focused on his goals, Prashant was able to make steady progress towards creating positive habits in his life.

Self-reflection was also an important aspect of Prashant's habit change journey. He regularly checked in with himself to assess how he was feeling and what triggers or obstacles he was facing. This allowed him to adjust his approach as needed and stay on track towards his goals.

Overall, by applying the science of habit formation to his own life and staying committed to the process, Prashant was able to make lasting changes that improved his health and well-being. He understood that changing habits is a lifelong journey, and that the key to success is to remain patient, persistent, and self-aware.

The Science of Habit Formation:

Habit formation is a process that involves three stages: the cue, the routine, and the reward. The cue is a trigger that initiates the habit, the routine is the behaviour itself, and the reward is the outcome that reinforces the habit. For example, if you have a habit of snacking on junk food in the afternoon, the cue might be feeling hungry or stressed, the routine might be reaching for a bag of chips, and the reward might be the pleasure you get from eating them.

According to the science of habit formation, the more frequently you repeat this cycle, the stronger the habit becomes. The habit loop creates neural pathways in your brain that make the behaviour automatic, which means you don't have to think about it consciously. This is why habits can be hard to break, and why forming new habits can be challenging.

The science of habit formation is a field of study that explores the cognitive and neurological processes involved in the formation of habits. Scientists have identified several key elements that are essential for habit formation, including cues, routines, and rewards.

Cues are the triggers that initiate a habit. They can be anything from a time of day to a specific location or feeling. For example, the sound of an alarm clock in the morning may be a cue to get out of bed and start the day. The sight of a gym bag may be a cue to go to the gym.

Routines are the actual behaviours that make up a habit. They can be anything from brushing your teeth to going for a run or checking your email.

Rewards are the positive outcomes that result from performing a habit. They can be anything from a sense of accomplishment to a physical reward like a piece of chocolate.

How to Make New Habits Stick:

Fortunately, there are strategies you can use to make new habits stick. Here are some tips:

- **Start Small:** One of the reasons people fail to form new habits is because they try to do too much at once. Instead, start small and focus on one habit at a time. For example, if you want to start exercising, begin by doing just five minutes of exercise a day and gradually increase the duration over time.

- **Choose the Right Cue:** To form a new habit, you need to have a cue that triggers the behavior. Choose a cue that is easy to remember and that you encounter frequently. For example, if you want to start flossing your teeth, use brushing your teeth as the cue.

- **Make it Easy:** Make the habit as easy as possible to perform. For example, if you want to start meditating, choose a time and place where you won't be interrupted and where you can sit comfortably. If you make the habit too difficult, you're more likely to give up.

- **Reward Yourself:** The reward is a crucial part of the habit loop, so make sure to reward yourself when you perform the behavior. The reward doesn't have to be big or expensive; it could be as simple as giving yourself a pat on the back or a few minutes of relaxation.

- **Track Your Progress:** Tracking your progress can help you stay motivated and see how far you've come. Use a habit tracker app or a journal to record your progress and celebrate your successes.

- **Stay Consistent:** Consistency is key when it comes to forming new habits. Try to perform the behaviour at the same time every day, and don't skip a day. The more consistent you are, the stronger the habit will become.

Habits are an essential part of our lives, and forming new habits can be challenging. However, by understanding the science of habit formation and using the strategies outlined in this chapter, you can make new habits stick. Start small, choose the right cue, make it easy, reward yourself, track your progress, and stay consistent, and you'll be well on your way to forming new habits that will benefit your life.

Key points to remember :

- Habits are formed through a three-step process: cue, routine, and reward.
- Cues can be internal or external triggers that prompt the habit.
- Routines are the actions that make up the habit.
- Rewards are the positive outcomes that reinforce the habit.
- The basal ganglia in the brain is responsible for the formation of habits.
- Habits can be changed by identifying and modifying the cues, routines, and rewards.
- To make new habits stick, it's important to start small and be consistent.
- It takes an average of 66 days for a new habit to become automatic.

- Habit stacking, or adding a new habit to an existing one, can make it easier to adopt.
- Visualisation and positive self-talk can help reinforce new habits.

Remember, habits are formed through repeated actions and positive reinforcement, so it's important to be patient and consistent when trying to develop new habits. Understanding the science of habit formation can help you create lasting change in your life.

Chapter 4: Breaking Bad Habits: Strategies for Overcoming Temptation and Weakness

Prashant had identified his bad habits and understood the science behind habit formation. But he still struggled with breaking his bad habits. Whenever he tried to resist a bad habit, he found himself giving in to temptation and weakness. He realized that he needed to develop strategies to overcome these obstacles if he wanted to make lasting changes.

The first strategy Prashant employed was to identify his triggers. He knew that certain cues, such as stress or boredom, would often lead him to engage in his bad habits. By recognizing these triggers, he could avoid or prepare for them, reducing the likelihood of falling into old patterns. For instance, he started keeping healthy snacks nearby when he knew he would be under stress at work, rather than reaching for the junk food in the vending machine.

The second strategy Prashant used was to replace his bad habits with healthier alternatives. Instead of turning to social media or Netflix when he was feeling overwhelmed, he started taking a walk or practicing yoga. He found that these activities not only helped him to resist temptation, but also improved his overall mood and well-being.

The third strategy Prashant employed was to enlist the support of friends and family. He shared his goals with those closest to him, and they held him accountable. They would encourage him when he was feeling discouraged and celebrate his successes. Prashant also joined a support group for people trying to break bad habits, where he could share his experiences and learn from others.

The fourth strategy Prashant used was to practice mindfulness. By being present in the moment and fully aware of his thoughts and feelings, he could better resist temptation and avoid slipping back into bad habits. He started practicing mindfulness techniques like deep breathing, meditation, and yoga, which helped him to stay focused and centered throughout the day.

The final strategy Prashant employed was to reward himself for his successes. Every time he resisted a bad habit or engaged in a healthier alternative, he would reward himself with something he enjoyed, like a favorite meal or a movie night with friends. These rewards helped him to stay motivated and reminded him of the progress he had made.

Prashant found that by using these strategies together, he was able to overcome temptation and weakness and break his bad habits. He felt more in control of his life and more confident in his ability to make lasting changes.

Breaking bad habits can be a challenging task, as they are deeply ingrained behaviors that have become automatic responses to specific situations or triggers. It is essential to overcome these habits as they can have negative consequences on your physical and mental health, relationships, and overall quality of life.

Habits are formed when we repeat an action in response to a particular cue, which leads to a reward. For example, when you feel stressed, you may reach for a cigarette, which provides temporary relief from the stress, and this behavior becomes a habit. Habits are difficult to break because they are wired into our brains, and the more we engage in a habit, the stronger the neural pathways become. However, it is possible to break bad habits and form new ones by understanding the underlying mechanisms of habit formation and adopting effective strategies.

Here are some strategies that can help you overcome temptation and weakness and break bad habits:

- **Identify your triggers**

  The first step in breaking a bad habit is to identify the triggers that lead to the habit. A trigger can be anything from a specific time of day, a particular place, a certain emotion, or even another person. For example, if you tend to snack when you are bored, then boredom is your trigger. By identifying your triggers, you can become more aware of your habits and start to develop strategies to overcome them.

- **Develop a replacement habit**

  One effective way to break a bad habit is to replace it with a new, positive habit. For example, if you tend to reach for a cigarette when you feel stressed, try replacing that habit with a healthier alternative, such as taking a walk or practicing deep breathing. The new habit should provide a similar reward to the old habit, but with a more positive outcome. The key is to make the replacement habit easy to do and to repeat it consistently until it becomes automatic.

- **Use positive affirmations**

Positive affirmations are statements that help to reinforce positive behaviors and beliefs. By using positive affirmations, you can rewire your brain and create new neural pathways that support the new habit you are trying to develop. For example, if you are trying to quit smoking, you might repeat the affirmation "I am a non-smoker" to yourself several times a day. Over time, this positive affirmation can help to strengthen your resolve and make it easier to resist the temptation to smoke.

- **Build a support system**

Breaking a bad habit can be challenging, and it is essential to have a support system in place to help you stay on track. Your support system can be made up of friends, family, or a support group that shares your goal. They can provide encouragement, accountability, and a sounding board when you need to talk through challenges or setbacks.

- **Practice mindfulness**

  Mindfulness is the practice of being present and aware of your thoughts, feelings, and physical sensations without judgment. By practicing mindfulness, you can develop greater self-awareness, which can help you to identify your triggers and develop strategies to overcome them. Mindfulness can also help you to manage stress and improve your overall well-being, which can make it easier to break bad habits.

- **Reward yourself**

  It is essential to reward yourself for making progress in breaking a bad habit. Rewards can provide motivation and reinforce positive behaviors. However, it is important to choose rewards that are consistent with the new habit you are trying to form. For example, if you are trying to eat healthier, you might reward yourself with a new cookbook or a healthy meal at your favorite restaurant.

- **Practice self-compassion**

  Breaking a bad habit can be a challenging process, and it is essential to practice self-compassion along the way. Be kind to yourself and acknowledge that setbacks and challenges are a natural part of the process. Instead of beating yourself up for slipping up, use the experience as an opportunity to learn and develop new strategies to overcome the temptation in the future. Remember that breaking a habit is a journey, and progress is not always linear.

- **Make a plan**

  Developing a plan can help you to stay on track and manage potential obstacles. Your plan should include specific goals and strategies for achieving them. For example, if you are trying to quit smoking, your plan might include identifying triggers, finding replacement habits, building a support system, and using positive affirmations. By breaking down your goals into manageable steps, you can stay motivated and focused on your progress.

- **Track your progress**

  Tracking your progress can help you to stay motivated and see the positive changes that are happening as you break your bad habit. You can track your progress by using a habit tracker or journal, where you can record your successes and challenges. By reviewing your progress regularly, you can identify areas where you are making progress and where you need to focus more effort.

- **Stay committed**

  Breaking a bad habit requires commitment and consistency. It is essential to stay focused on your goals and not give up when you experience setbacks. Remember that breaking a habit is a process, and it may take time to see significant changes. Be patient and stay committed to your plan, and over time, you will start to see the positive results.

Breaking bad habits can be a challenging process, but by adopting effective strategies and staying committed to your goals, it is possible to overcome temptation and weakness and create positive, lasting change. Remember to be kind to yourself, celebrate your successes, and seek support when you need it. With time and effort, you can break any bad habit and develop new, positive habits that support your overall health and well-being.

Let's take the example of alcoholism. A trigger for alcohol consumption may be social situations or feeling overwhelmed by stress. The cue of being in social situations or feeling stressed triggers the habit of drinking, and the reward is the temporary relief or relaxation that alcohol provides. Over time, this habit becomes deeply ingrained, and the brain associates being in social situations or feeling stressed with the need to drink.

To break this habit, it is important to identify the triggers and develop strategies to manage stress and social situations in healthier ways. This can include things like seeking out support from friends or family, finding alternative ways to relax such as exercise or hobbies, or seeking help from a therapist or addiction specialist. It may also involve making changes to your social circle, avoiding situations or people that trigger the habit, and finding new ways to socialize that don't involve drinking. By identifying the triggers and developing alternative behaviors, you can start to break the association between social situations or stress and drinking, making it easier to overcome the habit of alcohol consumption.

Some examples:

1. Breaking the habit of smoking: Someone who is trying to quit smoking can use a variety of strategies to overcome temptation and weakness. For example, they could replace the habit of smoking with a healthier habit, like going for a walk or chewing gum. They could also avoid triggers that make them want to smoke, like social situations where others are smoking. Additionally, they could seek support from friends or join a support group to stay accountable and motivated.

2. Resisting the temptation to eat unhealthy food: Someone who wants to improve their diet and stop eating unhealthy food can use strategies like planning ahead, keeping healthy snacks on hand, and practicing mindful eating. They could also avoid keeping unhealthy food in the house or at their workplace, and make a

habit of reading food labels to make informed choices. Additionally, they could seek out support from friends or a nutritionist to help them stay on track.

3. Overcoming procrastination: Someone who struggles with procrastination can use strategies like breaking tasks down into smaller, manageable steps, using timers to stay focused, and setting deadlines for themselves. They could also eliminate distractions, like turning off notifications on their phone or finding a quiet workspace. Additionally, they could seek support from a mentor or coach to help them stay accountable and motivated.

4. Developing the habit of regular exercise: Someone who wants to develop the habit of regular exercise can use strategies like finding an enjoyable form of exercise, setting achievable goals, and making exercise a non-negotiable part of their daily routine. They could also seek out a workout buddy or join a fitness class to stay motivated and accountable. Additionally, they could track their progress and celebrate small milestones

along the way to maintain their momentum.

Key Points to Remember:

- Identify your triggers for bad habits and avoid or prepare for them
- Replace bad habits with healthier alternatives
- Enlist the support of friends and family
- Practice mindfulness to stay focused and centred
- Reward yourself for successes

Chapter 5: Developing Good Habits: Tips for Creating Positive Routines

Prashant had successfully overcome some of his bad habits, but he still wanted to cultivate more positive habits in his life. He had learned that habits were formed through repetition, so he set out to create positive routines that he could stick to.

Here are some tips for developing good habits and creating positive routines:

1. **Start Small:** Prashant had learned that trying to make big changes all at once could be overwhelming and lead to failure. Instead, he started with small changes that were easy to incorporate into his daily routine. For example, he started by drinking a glass of water first thing in the morning, or doing a short meditation before bed. These small changes were easy to do consistently, and over time, they added up to big results.

2. **Set Goals:** Prashant knew that setting goals was an important part of habit formation. He set specific, measurable, and achievable goals for himself, such

as running for 10 minutes every day or reading for 30 minutes before bed. These goals helped him stay motivated and focused on his habits.

3. **Use Positive Reinforcement:** Prashant learned that positive reinforcement was a powerful tool for habit formation. He rewarded himself whenever he successfully completed a habit, such as treating himself to a healthy snack or buying a new book. This positive reinforcement helped him associate his habits with positive feelings and made it easier to stick to them.

4. **Create a Routine:** Prashant knew that creating a routine was key to habit formation. He created a daily schedule that included time for his habits, such as exercise or reading. This routine helped him make his habits a natural part of his day and eliminated the need for willpower and motivation.

5. **Find an Accountability Partner:** Prashant learned that having an accountability partner could be a powerful motivator for habit formation. He found a friend or family member

who also wanted to develop good habits, and they supported each other by checking in regularly and holding each other accountable for their progress.

6. **Be Mindful:** Prashant realized that being mindful was an important part of habit formation. He paid attention to his thoughts, feelings, and behaviors, and noticed when he was slipping into old habits or negative patterns. This mindfulness helped him catch himself before he fell back into his old ways and allowed him to make conscious choices about his behavior.

7. **Focus on the Process, Not the Outcome:** Prashant learned that focusing on the process of habit formation was more important than the outcome. He focused on the small steps he could take each day to form his habits, rather than worrying about achieving a specific result. This helped him stay motivated and make steady progress towards his goals.

By applying these tips and strategies, Prashant was able to develop new positive habits and create a more fulfilling and productive life for himself. He knew that habits were a powerful tool for personal growth and was excited to see where his newfound habits would take him.

Developing good habits is essential for maintaining a healthy, happy life. Habits are the routines that we engage in daily, and they can have a significant impact on our physical, mental, and emotional well-being. Developing positive habits can help us to improve our health, relationships, productivity, and overall quality of life. In this section, we will explore some tips for creating positive routines that can help you to develop good habits.

- **Identify your goals**

  The first step in developing good habits is to identify your goals. What do you want to achieve? Do you want to improve your fitness, relationships, or career? Once you have identified your goals, you can start to create habits that support those goals. For example, if your goal is to improve your fitness, you might develop a habit of going to the gym every morning.

- **Start small**

  When developing new habits, it is essential to start small. Trying to change too much at once can be overwhelming and can lead to failure. Instead, start with one small habit that you can realistically stick to. For example, if your goal is to start exercising more, you might start with a daily walk around your neighborhood. By starting small, you can build momentum and gradually develop more significant habits over time.

- **Be consistent**

  Consistency is essential when developing good habits. It is important to engage in your new habit consistently, whether it is daily, weekly, or monthly. This consistency helps to reinforce the habit and make it more automatic. For example, if you are trying to develop a habit of meditation, you might start with a 5-minute session every morning and gradually increase the time over time. Consistently engaging in the habit helps to make it a part of your routine and makes it easier to maintain over time.

- **Use positive reinforcement**

  Positive reinforcement is an effective way to reinforce good habits. Rewarding yourself for engaging in your new habit can help to reinforce the behavior and make it more automatic. For example, if your habit is to exercise every morning, you might reward yourself with a healthy breakfast or a relaxing shower after your workout. These rewards can help to reinforce the habit and make it more enjoyable.

- **Eliminate distractions**

  Distractions can make it difficult to develop good habits. It is essential to identify and eliminate distractions that may interfere with your new routine. For example, if your habit is to read for 30 minutes every night, you might need to eliminate distractions such as television

  or social media. This can help you to stay focused on your new habit and make it easier to stick to over time.

- **Develop a support system**

  Having a support system can be incredibly helpful when developing new habits. Surround yourself with people who support your goals and encourage you to stick to your new routines. This can include friends, family members, or a professional coach. Having a support system can help you to stay motivated and overcome any obstacles that may arise.

- **Track your progress**

  Tracking your progress is an effective way to stay motivated and see the positive changes that are happening as you develop new habits. You can track your progress by using a habit tracker or journal, where you can record your successes and challenges. By reviewing your progress regularly, you can identify areas where you are making progress and where you need to focus more effort.

- **Be patient**

  Developing good habits takes time, and it is important to be patient with yourself. Habits are formed through repetition, and it may take weeks or even months to develop new routines. Be kind to yourself and celebrate your successes along the way. Remember that developing positive habits is a journey, and progress is not always linear.

Developing good habits is essential for maintaining a healthy, happy life. By identifying your goals, starting small, being consistent.

Key points to remember :

- Start small: Develop small, achievable goals for creating new habits.

- Focus on consistency: Make sure to repeat the behavior consistently to turn it into a habit.

- Establish a cue: Connect the new habit with an existing routine to help form a strong connection.

- Create a supportive environment: Remove any obstacles and distractions that may hinder the formation of the new habit.

- Reward yourself: Celebrate the small wins to keep yourself motivated and encouraged.
- Use positive self-talk: Encourage yourself with positive affirmations to boost confidence and self-esteem.
- Keep track of progress: Monitor and track your progress to help stay accountable and motivated.
- Develop a routine: Incorporate the new habit into a daily routine to help make it a natural part of your day.
- Embrace failure: Don't be discouraged by setbacks, they are a natural part of the habit-forming process.
- Seek support: Build a support network of family, friends or colleagues to help stay motivated and accountable.

Remember that habit formation is a gradual process that requires patience, persistence, and self-reflection. With the right mindset and approach, you can create positive habits that improve your health, productivity, and overall well-being.

Chapter 6 : Maintaining Good Habits: How to Stay on Track

Prashant had realized that maintaining new positive habits is just as important as developing them in the first place. He had experienced the difficulty of breaking old bad habits and forming new good habits. But he also knew that the hard work was not over yet. To keep his new positive habits alive, he needed to implement strategies that would help him stay on track.

One of the most important strategies for maintaining good habits is to create a supportive environment. Prashant knew that his environment plays a significant role in shaping his behavior, so he made sure to surround himself with people who support his new positive habits. He also made changes to his physical environment, such as keeping healthy snacks on hand and creating a designated exercise space in his home.

Another key strategy is to track progress and celebrate small wins. Prashant continued to use his habit journal to track his progress and note any setbacks. But he also learned to celebrate small victories along the way. By acknowledging and celebrating even the smallest achievements, he felt motivated to continue with his new positive habits.

Prashant also learned the importance of self-care. He realized that taking care of his physical and mental health was essential for maintaining his new positive habits. This included getting enough sleep, taking breaks when he needed them, and finding healthy ways to manage stress.

Additionally, Prashant understood the power of accountability. He shared his new positive habits with his family and friends and even joined a support group of like-minded individuals. Having someone to hold him accountable and provide encouragement when he felt discouraged made a significant difference in his ability to maintain his new positive habits.

Lastly, Prashant knew that setbacks were inevitable, and it was essential to have a plan for how to handle them. He learned that slipping up on his new positive habits didn't mean he had failed, and it was crucial to get back on track as soon as possible. He created a plan for how to deal with setbacks and practiced self-compassion when things didn't go as planned.

- **Keep Track of Your Progress**

  One of the most effective ways to maintain good habits is to track your progress. This helps you to stay motivated and see the positive changes that are happening in your life. Prashant continued to use his habit journal to track his daily routines and habits. He also made a point to celebrate his progress and give himself credit for his accomplishments.

- **Find an Accountability Partner**

  Another powerful strategy for staying on track is to find an accountability partner. This can be a friend, family member, or even a coach or mentor who can help you stay committed to your goals. Prashant reached out to a friend who was also trying to develop positive habits in his life. They became each other's accountability partners, checking in regularly and offering support and encouragement.

- **Plan for Obstacles**

  Even with the best intentions and strategies, there will always be obstacles that can derail your progress. Prashant learned to anticipate these obstacles and plan for them in advance. For example, he knew that he tended to snack on unhealthy foods when he was stressed at work. So, he started packing healthy snacks and taking breaks to stretch or walk around the office when he felt stressed.

- **Stay Flexible and Adaptable**

  While it's important to have a plan, it's also important to stay flexible and adaptable. Life is unpredictable, and sometimes unexpected events can throw a wrench in your plans. Prashant learned to be patient and flexible when things didn't go according to plan. He also reminded himself that setbacks and failures are a natural part of the process, and that he could always get back on track.

- **Focus on the Process, Not the Outcome**

  One of the biggest challenges in maintaining good habits is staying focused on the process, rather than the outcome. It's easy to get discouraged if you don't see immediate results, or if you don't achieve your goals as quickly as you had hoped. Prashant learned to focus on the small daily actions that led to his success, rather than obsessing over the end result.

- **Celebrate Your Successes**

  Finally, Prashant learned the importance of celebrating his successes along the way. Even small accomplishments are worth celebrating, as they help to keep you motivated and reinforce the positive changes you are making in your life. Prashant made a point to celebrate his successes, whether it was treating himself to a favorite meal or taking a day off to relax and recharge.

By focusing on these strategies, Prashant was able to maintain his good habits and continue to make progress towards his goals. He learned that developing positive habits is not a one-time event, but rather an ongoing process of growth and self-improvement. With patience, persistence, and a commitment to his own well-being, he knew that he could achieve anything he set his mind to.

Examples:

1. Make a commitment to yourself: One practical example of this strategy is making a commitment to exercise for at least 30 minutes every day. You can make a commitment to yourself by setting a specific goal and writing it down. For example, you can write, "I will exercise for 30 minutes every day for the next 30 days." This will help you stay focused and motivated to stick to your habit.

2. Build a support system: A practical example of building a support system is joining a fitness class or a running club. This will not only help you stay accountable to your habit, but it will also provide you with a community of people who share your goals and can offer encouragement and support.

3. Create reminders: A practical example of creating reminders is setting an alarm or reminder on your phone to remind you to meditate every day. You can also place visual reminders around your home or workplace to help you stay focused on your habit. For example, you can place a sticky note on your fridge that says, "Drink water before every meal."

4. Track your progress: A practical example of tracking your progress is keeping a journal or using an app to track your food intake or daily exercise. This will help you see how far you've come and motivate you to keep going.

5. Celebrate your successes: A practical example of celebrating your successes is treating yourself to a massage or a movie after completing a month of consistent exercise or healthy eating. Celebrating your successes will help you stay motivated and reinforce the positive impact of your good habits.

Key points to remember:

- Habits are not a one-time event, but a lifelong process.
- Maintaining good habits requires consistency and discipline.
- Accountability can be a powerful tool in maintaining good habits.
- Visual cues and reminders can help reinforce good habits.
- It's important to be flexible and adaptable in adjusting habits to fit changing circumstances.
- Celebrating successes, no matter how small, can help reinforce good habits.
- Keeping a positive mindset and focusing on the benefits of good habits can help overcome challenges and setbacks.
- Regularly reflecting on progress and re-evaluating habits can help identify areas for improvement and prevent backsliding.

- It's okay to seek support from others, whether it's through a coach, mentor, or accountability partner.

- Making good habits a priority and incorporating them into daily routines can lead to long-term success and improved well-being.

Chapter 7: Staying Accountable: The Importance of Tracking and Measuring Progress

Prashant discovers the importance of tracking and measuring his progress in order to maintain his positive habits. He realizes that keeping track of his progress not only helps him stay accountable to himself, but it also provides motivation and a sense of accomplishment.

Prashant learns that tracking progress can be done in a variety of ways, such as using a habit tracking app, journaling, or creating a visual representation of progress. He also understands that measuring progress can be done through quantitative or qualitative methods, depending on the nature of the habit.

Prashant begins to implement these strategies by using a habit tracking app on his phone. He inputs his positive habits and sets reminders for himself to complete them each day. He also creates a visual representation of his progress by drawing a calendar and filling in each day that he successfully completes his habits. This provides him with a tangible representation of his progress and keeps him motivated to continue.

Prashant also realizes the importance of celebrating small victories along the way. He understands that progress isn't always linear, and that setbacks may happen. However, by focusing on the positive progress he has made and celebrating small victories, he is able to stay motivated and keep his positive habits alive.

Overall, Prashant learns that staying accountable to himself and tracking his progress is essential for maintaining his positive habits over the long term. By implementing strategies such as habit tracking apps, visual representations of progress, and celebrating small victories, he is able to stay on track and continue living a healthier and more fulfilling life.

Accountability is a crucial component of personal and professional growth. When individuals take ownership of their goals and track their progress, they are more likely to stay motivated and achieve their desired outcomes. Tracking and measuring progress are effective ways to stay accountable, and they provide valuable insights into the effectiveness of a particular approach. In this essay, I will discuss the importance of staying accountable, the benefits of tracking and measuring progress, and strategies for effective accountability.

Importance of Staying Accountable:

Accountability means taking ownership of one's actions and decisions. When individuals hold themselves accountable, they are more likely to achieve their goals and take responsibility for their outcomes. Staying accountable also helps individuals stay focused on their goals, avoid distractions and setbacks, and improve their performance. Additionally, accountability helps individuals identify areas for improvement and take corrective actions to achieve better results.

Benefits of Tracking and Measuring Progress:

Tracking and measuring progress are essential for staying accountable. These practices provide valuable insights into the effectiveness of a particular approach and help individuals stay motivated to achieve their goals. Here are some specific benefits of tracking and measuring progress:

1. **Visibility:** When individuals track and measure their progress, they can see their progress over time. This visibility helps them stay motivated and see the positive results of their efforts, which

can be an excellent source of motivation.

2. **Feedback:** Tracking and measuring progress provide feedback on the effectiveness of specific behaviors and strategies. This feedback can help individuals adjust their approach and make more informed decisions about how to achieve their goals.

3. **Motivation:** When individuals see progress towards their goals, they are more likely to stay motivated and committed to their efforts. This motivation can help them overcome challenges and setbacks, and ultimately achieve their desired outcomes.

4. **Accountability:** Tracking and measuring progress also help individuals stay accountable for their goals. When they see their progress or lack thereof, they can take corrective actions to improve their approach and achieve better results.

Strategies for Effective Accountability:

There are several strategies that individuals can use to stay accountable, track progress, and measure their performance effectively. Here are some specific strategies that can help individuals stay accountable:

1. **Set Specific and Measurable Goals:** Setting specific and measurable goals is the first step towards effective accountability. When individuals set goals, they have a clear target to work towards, and they can measure their progress towards that goal.

2. **Break Goals into Smaller Steps:** Breaking larger goals into smaller steps is an effective way to stay accountable. When individuals break goals into smaller, more manageable steps, they can see progress towards their larger goal and stay motivated to continue their efforts.

3. **Establish a Routine:** Establishing a routine is an effective way to form habits and stay accountable. When individuals establish a routine, they develop a consistent approach to

achieving their goals and are more likely to stay on track.

4. **Track Progress:** Tracking progress is an essential component of staying accountable. When individuals track their progress, they can see their progress over time, make adjustments to their approach, and stay motivated to continue their efforts.

5. **Celebrate Success:** Celebrating success is an effective way to stay motivated and stay accountable. When individuals celebrate their successes, they reinforce their positive behaviors and stay motivated to continue their efforts.

6. **Identify Obstacles:** Identifying obstacles is an effective way to stay accountable. When individuals identify obstacles that prevent them from achieving their goals, they can take corrective actions to overcome these obstacles and improve their performance.

Accountability is a critical component of personal and professional growth. When individuals hold themselves accountable, they are more likely to achieve their goals and take responsibility for their outcomes. Tracking and measuring progress are essential for staying accountable, and they provide valuable insights into the effectiveness of a particular approach. By setting specific and measurable goals, breaking goals into smaller steps, establishing a routine, tracking progress, celebrating success, and identifying obstacles, individuals can stay accountable and achieve their desired outcomes.

Tracking and measuring progress is essential for personal and professional growth. By monitoring progress, individuals can see how far they have come, identify areas for improvement, and stay motivated to continue their efforts.

Here are some reasons why tracking and measuring progress are important:

1. **Motivation:** When individuals track their progress, they can see how far they have come and stay motivated to continue their efforts. Seeing positive results can be a powerful source of motivation that encourages individuals to keep working towards their goals.

2. **Goal-setting:** Tracking progress can help individuals set specific and

measurable goals. By seeing their progress over time, individuals can set realistic goals and adjust their approach to achieve them.

3. **Accountability:** Tracking progress helps individuals stay accountable for their goals. When they see their progress, they can take corrective actions to improve their approach and achieve better results.

4. **Feedback:** Measuring progress provides feedback on the effectiveness of specific behaviors and strategies. This feedback can help individuals adjust their approach and make more informed decisions about how to achieve their goals.

5. **Time Management:** Tracking progress helps individuals manage their time more effectively. By monitoring their progress, they can identify tasks that take longer than expected and adjust their schedule accordingly.

6. **Improvement:** Tracking progress helps individuals identify areas for improvement. By seeing their progress

over time, individuals can identify patterns and areas where they need to improve their performance.

Overall, tracking and measuring progress are essential for achieving personal and professional goals. By adopting these practices, individuals can stay motivated, set realistic goals, stay accountable, make informed decisions, manage their time effectively, and improve their performance.

Tracking and measuring progress are essential for effective accountability. When individuals track their progress, they can see their progress over time, make adjustments to their approach, and stay motivated to continue their efforts. Additionally, tracking and measuring progress provide valuable feedback on the effectiveness of specific behaviors and strategies, and help individuals stay focused on their goals. By adopting strategies for effective accountability, individuals can stay on track, overcome challenges and setbacks, and ultimately achieve their desired outcomes.

Key points to remember:

- Tracking progress is important for maintaining positive habits

- Tracking progress can be done through habit tracking apps, journaling, or visual representations
- Measuring progress can be done through quantitative or qualitative methods
- Celebrating small victories along the way is essential for staying motivated and on track.

Chapter 8: Building a Support Network: The Power of Community in Habit Formation

Prashant had come a long way in his journey to build better habits, but he knew that he couldn't do it alone. He realized that having a supportive community could make all the difference in staying motivated and accountable.

Prashant began by reaching out to friends and family members who shared similar goals and interests. He found that having a group of people who understood what he was going through and could offer encouragement and advice was invaluable.

He also sought out online communities and forums dedicated to habit formation and self-improvement. These resources provided him with a wealth of knowledge and inspiration from people all around the world who were on the same journey.

But perhaps the most powerful source of support for Prashant was his accountability partner. He found a friend who was also working on building better habits and they agreed to check in with each other regularly to share progress and provide motivation. Knowing that he would have to report back to someone else on his progress made Prashant more committed to staying on track.

Prashant learned that building a support network doesn't just provide motivation and accountability, but it also creates a sense of community and belonging. Being part of a group of people who share similar goals and values can be incredibly empowering and motivating.

He also found that supporting others in their own journeys to build better habits was just as important as receiving support himself. By offering encouragement and advice to others, he felt a sense of purpose and fulfillment that reinforced his own commitment to his goals.

In summary, building a support network is a crucial component of successful habit formation. Whether it's through friends and family, online communities, or accountability partners, having a group of people to offer encouragement, advice, and accountability can make all the difference in achieving long-term success.

Habit formation is a critical aspect of personal growth and development. It involves creating routines that help individuals achieve their goals and improve their lives. However, habit formation can be challenging, and it often requires a significant amount of effort and discipline. One way to make habit formation easier is by building a support network. A support network is a community of people who provide encouragement, motivation, and accountability as individuals work to form new habits.

Here are some reasons why building a support network is essential for habit formation:

1. **Provides Encouragement:** Forming new habits can be difficult, and setbacks can often leave individuals feeling discouraged. A support network can provide encouragement and motivation when individuals are struggling to maintain their habits. Having people who believe in them can help individuals stay motivated and committed to their goals.

2. **Offers Accountability:** A support network can also provide accountability. When individuals have others who are holding them accountable, they are more likely to stick to their habits. Knowing that someone else is tracking their progress can motivate individuals to

continue working towards their goals, even when they are feeling unmotivated.

3. **Shares Knowledge and Experience:** A support network can also share knowledge and experience. Members of a support network may have experience with forming similar habits, and they can offer tips, tricks, and advice on how to overcome challenges and stick to their goals.

4. **Offers Emotional Support:** Building a support network can also provide emotional support. The journey of habit formation can be emotional, and having a community of people to turn to during challenging times can be immensely helpful. Members of a support network can offer a listening ear, a word of encouragement, or even just a distraction when individuals are feeling overwhelmed or stressed.

5. **Reduces Isolation:** Habit formation can be a lonely journey, especially if individuals are making significant lifestyle changes. Building a support network can help individuals feel less isolated and more connected to others

who are working towards similar goals. Having a community of people who understand their struggles can help individuals feel less alone and more motivated to continue their efforts.

So, how can individuals build a support network to aid in habit formation?

1. **Identify Goals:** The first step in building a support network is to identify specific goals. Individuals need to identify what habits they want to form and why they want to form them. Once they have identified their goals, they can begin to seek out individuals who share similar goals and interests.

2. **Join Groups and Communities:** Joining groups and communities is a great way to build a support network. Individuals can join online groups, local meetups, or even start their own groups to connect with like-minded individuals. These groups provide opportunities to share experiences, exchange advice, and offer encouragement.

3. **Find an Accountability Partner:** An accountability partner is someone who

can hold individuals accountable for their habits. This person can be a friend, family member, or even a coach. An accountability partner can check in regularly to see how individuals are progressing with their habits and offer support when they are struggling.

4. **Share Progress:** Sharing progress with others is an excellent way to build a support network. By sharing progress, individuals can receive feedback, encouragement, and motivation to keep working towards their goals. Social media is an excellent platform for sharing progress and connecting with others who are working towards similar goals.

5. **Attend Classes and Workshops:** Attending classes and workshops is another way to build a support network. These events provide opportunities to meet new people who are interested in similar topics and can offer guidance and support.

In conclusion, building a support network is a powerful way to aid in habit formation. A support network can provide encouragement, accountability, knowledge and experience, emotional support, and reduce isolation. By identifying goals, joining groups and communities, finding an accountability partner, sharing progress, and attending classes and workshops, individuals can build a strong support network that will help them stay on track with their habit formation goals. Habits are not formed in isolation, and having a support network can make the journey more manageable, enjoyable, and ultimately successful.

Here are some additional tips for building a support network for habit formation:

1. **Choose the Right People:** When building a support network, it's essential to choose the right people. Individuals should seek out individuals who are supportive, positive, and have similar goals and interests. The support network should consist of people who will provide constructive feedback and offer encouragement when needed.

2. **Be Open and Honest:** It's crucial to be open and honest when building a support network. Individuals should share their goals and progress openly

with others. This will help to build trust and create a safe space for individuals to discuss their struggles and successes.

3. **Give Back:** Building a support network is a two-way street. Individuals should be willing to offer support to others as well. By giving back and providing encouragement to others, individuals can create a sense of community and help others achieve their goals.

4. **Stay Committed:** Building a support network takes time and effort. Individuals should stay committed to building relationships and supporting others. It's essential to be consistent in attending meetings, following up with accountability partners, and showing support to others.

5. **Celebrate Success:** Celebrating success is an important part of building a support network. Individuals should take the time to celebrate their progress and successes with others. This will help to build momentum and motivation and inspire others to continue working towards their goals.

In conclusion, building a support network is a powerful tool for habit formation. It can provide encouragement, accountability, knowledge and experience, emotional support, and reduce isolation. By identifying goals, joining groups and communities, finding an accountability partner, sharing progress, attending classes and workshops, choosing the right people, being open and honest, giving back, staying committed, and celebrating success, individuals can build a strong support network that will help them stay on track with their habit formation goals.

Key points to remember:

1. Having a support network is important for habit formation because it provides accountability and motivation.

2. Prashant joined a gym and made friends with people who shared his interest in fitness. They encouraged each other to stay on track with their workout routines.

3. Online communities can also be a valuable source of support, particularly for people with niche interests or goals.

4. Social media platforms can be a double-edged sword when it comes to habit formation. While they can provide a sense of community and motivation, they can also be a distraction and a source of comparison and negativity.

5. It's important to be intentional about the type of community you surround yourself with. Seek out people who share your values and goals, and who will support you in your efforts to build positive habits.

6. Being part of a support network is not just about receiving help and encouragement, but also about giving it. By being a positive influence on others, you can strengthen your own commitment to your goals.

7. Building a support network takes time and effort, but the benefits are well worth it. With the right people in your corner, you can overcome obstacles,

stay accountable, and achieve lasting success in habit formation.

Chapter 9: The Mind-Body Connection: How Physical Health Impacts Habits

Prashant had always thought of his mind and body as separate entities. He believed that his mental and emotional health were important, but he didn't place the same emphasis on his physical health. However, as he learned more about the science of habit formation, he realized that the mind and body are deeply connected, and that taking care of his physical health was essential for building and maintaining good habits.

Research has shown that physical exercise can have a significant impact on the brain and its ability to form and maintain new habits. Exercise has been shown to increase the production of brain-derived neurotrophic factor (BDNF), a protein that is essential for neuroplasticity, or the brain's ability to change and adapt. Neuroplasticity is critical for habit formation, as it allows the brain to form new neural pathways that support new behaviors and routines.

In addition to the benefits for the brain, physical exercise can also have a direct impact on the body's ability to form and maintain habits. Exercise has been shown to increase self-regulation, or the ability to control one's behavior and resist temptation. This is essential for breaking bad habits and developing new positive routines.

Prashant began to incorporate physical exercise into his daily routine, starting with small activities like taking a brisk walk or doing some gentle yoga. As he became more active, he noticed that he had more energy and felt more motivated to stick to his positive habits. He also found that exercise helped him to manage stress and reduce his reliance on unhealthy coping mechanisms like overeating or social media scrolling.

But physical exercise is not the only aspect of physical health that can impact habit formation. Nutrition is also critical for building and maintaining good habits. The foods we eat can impact our energy levels, mood, and cognitive function, all of which can impact our ability to form and maintain habits. Prashant began to pay more attention to his diet, focusing on whole foods like fruits, vegetables, lean proteins, and whole grains, while limiting his intake of processed and sugary foods.

Sleep is another critical aspect of physical health that can impact habit formation. Getting enough sleep is essential for cognitive function, energy levels, and emotional regulation, all of which are important for forming and maintaining positive habits. Prashant began to prioritize his sleep, setting a regular bedtime and creating a bedtime routine to help him unwind and relax before bed.

By taking care of his physical health, Prashant was able to support his mental and emotional well-being, making it easier to form and maintain positive habits. He also found that his physical health and mental health were deeply interconnected, and that making changes in one area could have a significant impact on the other.

The mind-body connection is the link between the physical and mental aspects of our well-being. It is the idea that the health of our body affects the health of our mind and vice versa. The mind-body connection is essential to understanding how physical health impacts habits.

Habits are behaviors that are repeated over time and become automatic. They can be positive or negative, and they have a significant impact on our physical and mental health. Habits such as exercise, healthy eating, and good sleep patterns are positive habits that can improve physical and mental health. Negative habits such as smoking, excessive drinking, and poor diet can lead to physical and mental health problems.

Physical health is a crucial aspect of habit formation. The body's physical state influences the mind's ability to form and maintain habits. The following are some ways physical health impacts habits:

1. **Energy levels:** Physical health plays a significant role in determining an individual's energy levels. People who have poor physical health often experience low energy levels, making it challenging to develop and maintain healthy habits. Low energy levels can make individuals feel lethargic, unmotivated, and unwilling to engage in physical activities.

2. **Mental clarity:** Physical health also has a significant impact on mental clarity. People who are physically healthy often have better mental clarity and focus, making it easier to form and maintain habits. On the other hand, people who have poor physical health may experience brain fog, which can make it

difficult to concentrate and focus on forming habits.

3. **Sleep:** Sleep is essential to physical and mental health. People who are well-rested tend to have higher energy levels, better mental clarity, and a better ability to form and maintain healthy habits. On the other hand, individuals who do not get enough sleep often experience fatigue and lack of focus, making it difficult to develop and maintain healthy habits.

4. **Stress levels:** Physical health also impacts stress levels. People who are physically healthy often experience lower stress levels, making it easier to develop and maintain healthy habits. On the other hand, people who have poor physical health may experience high stress levels, which can make it challenging to form and maintain healthy habits.

5. **Motivation:** Physical health has a significant impact on an individual's motivation to form and maintain healthy habits. People who are physically healthy often have higher motivation

levels, making it easier to stay committed to their goals. On the other hand, individuals who have poor physical health may experience low motivation levels, making it difficult to form and maintain healthy habits.

To elaborate further, the physical and mental aspects of our well-being are deeply interconnected. Our physical health affects our mental health, and our mental health affects our physical health. Therefore, when it comes to habit formation, taking care of our physical health is critical for success.

Physical health impacts habits by influencing factors such as energy levels, mental clarity, sleep, stress levels, and motivation. For example, someone who is experiencing low energy levels due to poor physical health may find it challenging to commit to a regular exercise routine. Similarly, an individual experiencing brain fog or lack of focus due to poor physical health may find it difficult to stick to a healthy eating plan or to make other positive changes.

Furthermore, sleep is crucial to physical and mental health. Individuals who are well-rested tend to have more energy, better mental clarity, and a better ability to form and maintain healthy habits. On the other hand, people who do not get enough sleep often experience fatigue and a lack of focus, making it difficult to develop and maintain healthy habits.

Stress levels also play a significant role in habit formation. Chronic stress can be detrimental to physical health and can cause mental health issues such as anxiety and depression. When an individual is experiencing high levels of stress, they may struggle to find the motivation to form and maintain healthy habits.

Finally, motivation is a crucial factor in habit formation. People who are motivated tend to stick to their goals and achieve positive results. Physical health affects motivation levels, and individuals who are physically healthy often have higher motivation levels, making it easier to stay committed to their goals. By contrast, people who are experiencing poor physical health may find it difficult to stay motivated and committed to their goals.

The mind-body connection is essential to understanding how physical health impacts habits. By taking care of our physical health, we can improve our mental health and increase our ability to form and maintain healthy habits.

Positive habits such as exercise, healthy eating, good sleep patterns, and stress reduction are critical to physical and mental health. By prioritizing physical health, we can improve our overall well-being and increase our ability to form and maintain healthy habits.

In conclusion, physical health plays a crucial role in habit formation. The body's physical state impacts an individual's ability to form and maintain habits. Low energy levels, mental fog, lack of focus, high stress levels, and low motivation levels are some of the ways poor physical health can impact habits. Positive habits such as exercise, healthy eating, and good sleep patterns are critical to physical and mental health. By prioritizing physical health, individuals can improve their overall well-being and increase their ability to form and maintain healthy habits.

Here are a few examples of how physical health impacts habit formation:

1. **Exercise and energy levels:** Exercise is an essential habit that can improve physical and mental health. However, it can be challenging to get started and stay committed to a regular exercise routine. One factor that can impact

exercise habits is energy levels. Individuals who are physically healthy and well-rested tend to have more energy, making it easier to commit to a regular exercise routine. On the other hand, people who are experiencing low energy levels due to poor physical health may find it difficult to stick to a regular exercise routine.

2. **Healthy eating and mental clarity:** A healthy diet is critical to physical and mental health. Eating a balanced diet that includes plenty of fruits, vegetables, whole grains, and lean protein can improve mental clarity and reduce brain fog. When an individual is experiencing mental clarity, they are better able to stay focused and motivated to form and maintain healthy habits.

3. **Sleep and stress reduction:** Sleep is essential to physical and mental health. Getting enough sleep can reduce stress levels, improve mental clarity, and increase energy levels. When an individual is well-rested, they are more likely to feel motivated to form and maintain healthy habits. On the other hand, people who do not get enough

sleep often experience fatigue and a lack of focus, making it challenging to develop and maintain healthy habits.

4. **Stress reduction and motivation:** Chronic stress can be detrimental to physical and mental health. When an individual is experiencing high levels of stress, they may struggle to find the motivation to form and maintain healthy habits. By reducing stress levels through practices such as meditation, yoga, or mindfulness, individuals can improve their ability to form and maintain healthy habits.

5. **Physical health and motivation:** Physical health impacts motivation levels. People who are physically healthy often have higher motivation levels, making it easier to stay committed to their goals. For example, someone who is experiencing chronic pain may find it difficult to commit to an exercise routine, while someone who is pain-free may find exercise more enjoyable and motivating. By prioritizing physical health, individuals can increase their motivation levels and

increase their ability to form and maintain healthy habits.

Key points to remember:

1. Physical health plays a crucial role in habit formation, as it directly impacts energy levels, mood, and motivation.

2. Exercise is a powerful tool for building good habits, as it releases endorphins and increases overall energy levels.

3. Sleep is another critical factor in habit formation, as lack of sleep can lead to decreased willpower and increased cravings for unhealthy habits.

4. Nutrition is also an important factor in habit formation, as a healthy diet can provide the necessary nutrients for optimal brain function and mood regulation.

5. Stress management is crucial for maintaining good habits, as stress can trigger unhealthy habits and hinder the development of new positive habits.

6. Mindfulness practices, such as meditation and deep breathing, can help

reduce stress and improve overall well-being, making it easier to maintain good habits.

7. Developing a balanced approach to physical health, including exercise, sleep, nutrition, and stress management, can create a strong foundation for habit formation and support long-term success.

Remember that the mind and body are interconnected, and taking care of your physical health can have a significant impact on your ability to form and maintain positive habits. Incorporating exercise, sleep, nutrition, stress management, and mindfulness practices into your daily routine can help create a strong foundation for successful habit formation.

Chapter 10: Cultivating Mental Resilience: Techniques for Overcoming Obstacles and Setbacks

After months of hard work, Prashant had developed a set of positive habits that had greatly improved his life. But he knew that there would still be obstacles and setbacks ahead, and he needed to be prepared to face them. He recognized that mental resilience was a crucial part of maintaining his good habits, and he began to cultivate techniques for building this resilience.

One of the first things Prashant learned was the importance of reframing his mindset. He realized that setbacks and failures were not necessarily indicators of his overall success or worth as a person. Instead, he began to view them as opportunities for growth and learning. By shifting his perspective in this way, he was able to bounce back more quickly from setbacks and avoid getting bogged down in negative self-talk.

Another technique that Prashant found helpful was mindfulness meditation. This practice involves sitting quietly and focusing on the present moment, without judgment or distraction. Through regular mindfulness meditation, Prashant was able to develop greater awareness of his thoughts and emotions, and he became better equipped to manage them when they threatened to derail his good habits.

In addition to mindfulness, Prashant also found value in cognitive behavioral therapy (CBT). This form of therapy helps individuals identify negative thought patterns and replace them with more positive ones. By using CBT techniques, Prashant was able to retrain his brain to focus on the positive aspects of his life and his progress, rather than dwelling on the negative.

Another important aspect of cultivating mental resilience is social support. Prashant recognized that he couldn't do everything on his own, and he sought out the help of friends and family members who could offer encouragement and accountability. By building a support network, Prashant was able to stay motivated and committed to his good habits, even during difficult times.

Finally, Prashant learned the value of self-compassion. He realized that he was only human, and that he was bound to make mistakes and experience setbacks. Rather than beating himself up over these setbacks, he learned to be kind and forgiving toward himself, and to treat himself with the same compassion and understanding that he would offer to a close friend.

Through these techniques and practices, Prashant was able to develop greater mental resilience and overcome obstacles and setbacks as they arose. He learned that building positive habits was not just about the habits themselves, but about the mindset and habits of mind that supported them. With these tools in his toolkit, Prashant was confident that he could maintain his good habits for years to come.

Mental resilience is the ability to cope with and overcome challenges, setbacks, and obstacles in life. Cultivating mental resilience is essential for maintaining a positive outlook, achieving goals, and living a fulfilling life. However, it can be challenging to develop and maintain mental resilience, especially in the face of adversity. This chapter will explore techniques for cultivating mental resilience and overcoming obstacles and setbacks.

1. **Embrace a Growth Mindset:**

A growth mindset is the belief that we can improve our abilities and overcome challenges through effort and perseverance. By embracing a growth mindset, we can cultivate mental resilience and overcome obstacles and setbacks. A growth mindset encourages us to view challenges as opportunities for growth and learning rather than failures.

To develop a growth mindset, we must focus on our effort and progress rather than our abilities and achievements. Instead of comparing ourselves to others or dwelling on our shortcomings, we should focus on our potential and what we can achieve through hard work and perseverance.

2. Practice Mindfulness:

Mindfulness is the practice of being present in the moment and non-judgmentally observing our thoughts and feelings. By practicing mindfulness, we can develop mental resilience by improving our ability to manage stress and anxiety.

To practice mindfulness, we should find a quiet and comfortable place to sit and focus on our breath. As we inhale and exhale, we should observe our thoughts and feelings without judgment. Whenever our mind wanders, we should gently bring our focus back to our breath.

3. Develop Positive Self-Talk:

Positive self-talk is the practice of using positive and empowering language to encourage ourselves and build mental resilience. By using positive self-talk, we can overcome obstacles and setbacks by reframing negative thoughts and beliefs.

To develop positive self-talk, we should identify negative thoughts and beliefs and replace them with positive and empowering ones. For example, if we experience a setback, we might tell ourselves, "This is an opportunity to learn and grow, and I am capable of overcoming this obstacle."

4. Build Social Support:

Social support is a crucial factor in cultivating mental resilience. By building social support, we can overcome obstacles and setbacks by seeking guidance, encouragement, and motivation from others.

To build social support, we should reach out to friends, family, or colleagues and share our challenges and setbacks with them. By seeking support from others, we can gain valuable insights and perspectives, receive encouragement and motivation, and feel less alone in our struggles.

5. Take Action:

Taking action is a critical factor in cultivating mental resilience. By taking action, we can overcome obstacles and setbacks by making progress toward our goals and building momentum.

To take action, we should set achievable goals and create an action plan to achieve them. We should break down our goals into smaller, manageable steps and take consistent action toward them. By taking action, we can build confidence, gain momentum, and cultivate mental resilience.

6. Develop Problem-Solving Skills:

Problem-solving skills are essential for overcoming obstacles and setbacks. By developing problem-solving skills, we can approach challenges with a clear and strategic mindset, enabling us to find solutions and overcome obstacles.

To develop problem-solving skills, we should practice breaking down complex problems into smaller, more manageable ones. We should identify potential solutions and evaluate their effectiveness, considering the pros and cons of each approach. By developing problem-solving skills, we can cultivate mental resilience and approach challenges with a strategic and effective mindset.

Examples of techniques for cultivating mental resilience and overcoming obstacles and setbacks include:

1. An example of embracing a growth mindset is the story of Michael Jordan, one of the greatest basketball players of all time. As a young athlete, Jordan faced many setbacks and failures, including being cut from his high school basketball team. However, he didn't let these setbacks define him or deter him from his goals. Instead, he embraced a growth mindset, working tirelessly to improve his skills and overcome obstacles. This mindset led him to achieve greatness and become an inspiration to others.

2. An example of practicing mindfulness is the story of Alex Honnold, a renowned rock climber. Honnold faces significant

challenges every time he climbs, including physical and mental challenges. To prepare for these challenges, he practices mindfulness, focusing on his breath and being present in the moment. By doing so, he is able to stay calm and focused during his climbs, enabling him to achieve incredible feats of athleticism.

3. An example of developing positive self-talk is the story of Nick Vujicic, a motivational speaker and author who was born without arms or legs. Despite facing significant obstacles and setbacks, Vujicic has developed a positive attitude and a belief in his own capabilities. He uses positive self-talk to encourage himself and overcome challenges, telling himself, "I can do this" and "I am capable of anything I set my mind to." Through this positive self-talk, Vujicic has been able to achieve incredible feats, including becoming a successful motivational speaker and author.

4. An example of building social support is the story of Oprah Winfrey, a media mogul and philanthropist. Throughout

her life, Winfrey has faced numerous obstacles and setbacks, including abuse, poverty, and racism. However, she has always had a strong support network, including her friends, family, and mentors. By seeking guidance, encouragement, and motivation from others, Winfrey has been able to overcome her obstacles and achieve her goals. She has also used her success to give back to others, creating a platform for positive change and inspiring others to overcome their own obstacles.

5. An example of taking action is the story of J.K. Rowling, the author of the Harry Potter series. Rowling faced many obstacles and setbacks on her path to becoming a successful author, including rejection letters and financial struggles. However, she didn't let these setbacks stop her from pursuing her dreams. Instead, she took action, writing every day and submitting her manuscript to publishers until it was accepted. By taking consistent action toward her goal, Rowling was able to achieve incredible success and inspire millions of readers around the world.

6. An example of developing problem-solving skills is the story of Elon Musk, the founder of Tesla and SpaceX. Musk faces significant challenges every day, including technological, financial, and regulatory challenges. To overcome these challenges, Musk has developed exceptional problem-solving skills, breaking down complex problems into smaller, more manageable ones and evaluating potential solutions. By doing so, he has been able to overcome obstacles and achieve remarkable success in the tech industry.

Cultivating mental resilience is essential for living a fulfilling and meaningful life. By embracing a growth mindset, practicing mindfulness, developing positive self-talk, building social support, taking action, and developing problem-solving skills, we can overcome obstacles and setbacks and achieve our goals. With these techniques, we can cultivate mental resilience and live a life of purpose and meaning.

Key points to remember:

1. Understand that setbacks are a natural part of the habit-forming process.

Accept them and use them as opportunities for growth and learning.

2. Develop a growth mindset, where you view challenges as opportunities to improve and learn, rather than as obstacles to be avoided.

3. Practice self-compassion and be kind to yourself when facing setbacks. Avoid self-criticism and negative self-talk.

4. Use positive affirmations to reframe your thoughts and beliefs about setbacks. Replace negative self-talk with positive, empowering statements.

5. Build a support system of friends, family, or a community who can provide encouragement and accountability.

6. Stay motivated and focused on your goals by regularly reviewing your progress and celebrating your successes.

7. Practice mindfulness and meditation to improve your mental resilience and ability to cope with stress.

8. Prioritize self-care by getting enough sleep, eating a healthy diet, and

exercising regularly. A healthy body can support a healthy mind and help you stay resilient in the face of challenges.

By implementing these techniques, you can cultivate the mental resilience needed to overcome obstacles and setbacks in your habit-forming journey. Remember to be patient with yourself and trust the process, and you will ultimately achieve your desired outcome.

Chapter 11: Mindfulness and Habit Formation: How to Practice Presence and Awareness

Prashant had been working hard to develop new positive habits and maintain them over the long term. However, he found that he was still struggling with distractions and mindlessness, which made it difficult for him to stay on track with his goals. This is when he discovered the power of mindfulness in habit formation.

Mindfulness is the practice of being fully present and aware of one's thoughts, feelings, and sensations in the moment. It involves paying attention to the present moment without judgment or distraction. Research has shown that mindfulness can be a powerful tool in habit formation, as it helps individuals to become more aware of their habits and the triggers that drive them.

Prashant started practicing mindfulness meditation regularly, which helped him to cultivate a greater sense of awareness and presence in his daily life. This, in turn, allowed him to recognize his habits more clearly and make conscious choices about whether to engage in them or not.

One of the key principles of mindfulness is non-judgment. When practicing mindfulness, one is encouraged to observe their thoughts and feelings without attaching judgment or meaning to them. This can be helpful when trying to break bad habits, as it allows individuals to view their thoughts and behaviors objectively, without getting caught up in feelings of shame or guilt.

Prashant also found that mindfulness helped him to reduce stress and anxiety, which are common triggers for bad habits. By practicing mindfulness, he was able to become more relaxed and centered, which made it easier for him to resist temptations and stay on track with his positive habits.

Another way that mindfulness can be helpful in habit formation is by fostering a sense of curiosity and openness. When practicing mindfulness, individuals are encouraged to approach their experiences with a sense of curiosity and openness, rather than preconceived ideas or judgments. This can be helpful when trying to develop new habits, as it allows individuals to explore different possibilities and approaches without getting stuck in rigid thinking patterns.

Overall, mindfulness can be a powerful tool in habit formation, as it helps individuals to become more aware of their thoughts, feelings, and behaviors in the present moment. By practicing mindfulness, individuals can cultivate a greater sense of presence and awareness, which can help them to break bad habits, develop new positive habits, and maintain them over the long term.

Mindfulness is the practice of being present and aware in the moment, with an attitude of openness and non-judgment. This practice has been shown to have numerous benefits for mental health, including reducing stress, anxiety, and depression. It can also be a powerful tool for habit formation, helping us to develop positive habits and break negative ones.

In this article, we will explore the ways in which mindfulness can support habit formation, and provide examples of how to practice mindfulness in your daily life.

1. Mindfulness and Habit Formation

Mindfulness can be a powerful tool for habit formation because it helps us to be more aware of our thoughts, feelings, and actions. This increased awareness allows us to make intentional choices about our behaviors, rather than simply reacting to our environment.

For example, if we are trying to form the habit of exercise, mindfulness can help us to notice the thoughts and feelings that arise when we consider going for a run. If we notice resistance or negative thoughts, we can use mindfulness techniques to observe these thoughts without judgment, and then choose to act in a way that aligns with our goals.

Similarly, mindfulness can help us to break negative habits by increasing our awareness of the triggers and rewards that underlie these behaviors. By bringing mindfulness to our negative habits, we can begin to notice the patterns that lead us to engage in these behaviors, and then make conscious choices to break the cycle.

2. How to Practice Mindfulness

There are many ways to practice mindfulness, but some of the most common techniques include:

a) Meditation

Meditation is a formal practice of mindfulness that involves sitting quietly and focusing on the breath or a specific object of attention. By bringing our attention to the present moment, we can develop greater awareness of our thoughts and feelings, and cultivate a sense of calm and clarity.

One example of a meditation technique for habit formation is the "craving surf" technique. This technique involves sitting quietly and observing the physical sensations that arise when we experience a craving for a particular behavior, such as smoking or overeating. By observing these sensations without judgment, we can develop greater awareness of the triggers that underlie our habits, and then make conscious choices to break the cycle.

b) Body Scan

A body scan is a mindfulness technique that involves bringing awareness to each part of the body, from head to toe. By tuning into the physical sensations of the body, we can develop greater awareness of our thoughts and emotions, and cultivate a sense of relaxation and grounding.

One example of a body scan technique for habit formation is the "habit loop scan." This technique involves scanning the body for physical sensations that arise when we engage in a particular behavior, such as biting our nails or scrolling social media. By bringing mindfulness to these physical sensations, we can begin to notice the patterns that lead us to engage in these behaviors, and then make conscious choices to break the cycle.

c) Mindful Breathing

Mindful breathing is a simple technique that involves focusing on the sensations of the breath as it enters and leaves the body. By bringing our attention to the present moment, we can develop greater awareness of our thoughts and emotions, and cultivate a sense of calm and relaxation.

One example of a mindful breathing technique for habit formation is the "urge surfing" technique. This technique involves focusing on the breath when we experience an urge to engage in a particular behavior, such as smoking or drinking. By bringing mindfulness to the breath, we can ride out the urge without giving in to the behavior.

d) Mindful Movement

Mindful movement involves bringing awareness to the physical sensations of the body as we engage in movement, such as yoga, walking, or stretching. By tuning into the body, we can develop greater awareness of our thoughts and emotions, and cultivate a sense of relaxation and grounding.

One example of a mindful movement technique for habit formation is the "habit replacement" technique. This technique involves engaging in a physical activity that replaces a negative habit, such as going for a walk instead of reaching for a cigarette. By bringing mindfulness to the physical sensations of the body during the activity, we can reinforce the positive habit and gradually break the negative one.

3. Tips for Practicing Mindfulness for Habit Formation

Here are some tips for incorporating mindfulness into your habit formation practice:

a) Start small

Mindfulness can be challenging to practice, especially at first. Start by incorporating short mindfulness exercises into your daily routine, such as a 5-minute body scan or a mindful breathing exercise.

b) Practice regularly

Consistency is key when it comes to mindfulness. Try to practice every day, even if it's just for a few minutes.

c) Notice your thoughts without judgement

Mindfulness is not about eliminating negative thoughts or emotions, but rather noticing them without judgement. When you notice negative thoughts or emotions arise, try to observe them without getting caught up in them.

d) Set intentions

Before engaging in a habit-forming activity, set an intention for how you want to behave. For example, if you're trying to break the habit of biting your nails, set an intention to notice when you're doing it and to replace the behavior with a mindful movement activity.

e) Be patient

Habit formation takes time, and mindfulness is no exception. Be patient with yourself and trust the process.

4. Conclusion

Mindfulness can be a powerful tool for habit formation, helping us to develop positive habits and break negative ones. By bringing mindfulness to our thoughts, emotions, and physical sensations, we can become more aware of our behavior and make intentional choices that support our goals. Mindful habits also have the potential to improve our overall well-being, reducing stress and increasing our sense of inner peace.

When incorporating mindfulness into your habit formation practice, it's important to remember that it takes time and consistent effort. Start small and gradually increase the amount of time you spend practicing mindfulness. Notice the thoughts and emotions that arise as you practice, and try to observe them without judgment. Remember that setbacks and obstacles are a natural part of the habit formation process, and approach them with a mindset of curiosity and self-compassion.

With practice and persistence, mindfulness can become a natural part of your habit formation process, leading to long-lasting changes that support your well-being and personal growth.

Key points to remember:

- Mindfulness is the practice of being present and fully engaged in the current moment.

- Mindfulness can be a powerful tool for habit formation because it helps to increase self-awareness and control over one's actions and reactions.

- Mindfulness can be practiced in various ways, including meditation, breathing exercises, and body scans.
- Consistent mindfulness practice can help individuals to better understand their habits and the triggers that drive them.
- Mindfulness can also help individuals to make more deliberate and intentional choices about their behavior.
- Combining mindfulness with other habit-forming strategies, such as cue, routine, and reward, can enhance the effectiveness of habit formation.
- Practicing mindfulness can also help individuals to cope with stress and setbacks, which are common obstacles in habit formation.
- Regular mindfulness practice can lead to improvements in overall well-being and mental health.

Chapter 12: Navigating Personal Growth: How Habits Can Help You Reach Your Potential

Prashant realized that developing good habits is not just about achieving a specific goal or improving one area of life. Rather, it is a tool for personal growth and reaching one's full potential. He understood that habits can impact all aspects of his life, from health and relationships to career and personal development.

Prashant began by setting ambitious goals for himself, such as learning a new language or taking on a leadership role in his job. He realized that developing positive habits would be key to achieving these goals, and that it would require consistent effort and self-discipline.

To help him stay on track, Prashant created a habit plan that included specific actions he needed to take each day to reach his goals. He also practiced mindfulness and self-reflection, which helped him stay present and aware of his thoughts and actions.

Through his journey of habit formation, Prashant discovered that habits can be powerful tools for personal growth and transformation. By focusing on developing positive habits and staying committed to his goals, he was able to overcome obstacles and achieve things he never thought possible.

For example, Prashant had always wanted to learn a new language but never found the time or motivation to do so. With his newfound understanding of habit formation, he created a daily habit of practicing the language for 30 minutes each day. Over time, this habit became a natural part of his routine, and he found that he was making progress and becoming more confident in his language skills.

Similarly, Prashant had always dreamed of taking on a leadership role in his job but felt overwhelmed by the prospect. By breaking down his goal into small, achievable habits, such as setting weekly goals and taking on additional responsibilities, he was able to build his confidence and eventually achieve his goal.

Through his experiences, Prashant learned that habits can be a powerful tool for personal growth and transformation. By setting ambitious goals, creating daily habits that support those goals, and practicing mindfulness and self-reflection, anyone can reach their full potential and live a fulfilling life.

Personal growth is a journey towards reaching one's full potential. It involves developing new skills, learning from experiences, and acquiring knowledge. One of the most important aspects of personal growth is building positive habits. Habits are routines that people develop over time, and they play a significant role in shaping their behavior and personality. In this essay, we will discuss how habits can help individuals reach their potential by explaining what habits are, how they work, and providing examples of how positive habits can transform individuals' lives.

Habits are automatic behaviors that people perform without conscious thought. They are formed through repetition and become ingrained in a person's mind and body. Habits can be either positive or negative. Positive habits are behaviors that lead to positive outcomes, while negative habits are behaviors that lead to negative outcomes. Positive habits can be developed and strengthened through intentional practice, while negative habits can be unlearned and replaced with positive ones.

How Do Habits Work?

Habits are formed through a loop that includes a cue, a routine, and a reward. The cue is a trigger that initiates the behavior, the routine is the behavior itself, and the reward is the outcome that reinforces the behavior. When a behavior is repeated in response to a specific cue, the loop becomes stronger, and the behavior becomes more automatic. Over time, the behavior becomes a habit, and the cue is no longer necessary to initiate the behavior. This is why habits can be so powerful; they become automatic, and individuals don't need to rely on willpower to maintain the behavior.

Examples of Positive Habits:

There are many positive habits that individuals can develop to help them reach their potential. Some examples include:

Exercise: Regular exercise is a positive habit that can lead to physical and mental health benefits. Exercise has been shown to reduce stress, increase energy levels, and improve cognitive function. Developing the habit of exercising regularly can help individuals reach their physical potential and improve their mental well-being.

Reading: Reading is a positive habit that can increase knowledge, improve cognitive function, and reduce stress. Developing the habit of reading regularly can help individuals expand their horizons and reach their intellectual potential.

Goal Setting: Setting goals is a positive habit that can help individuals achieve their ambitions. By setting specific, measurable, achievable, relevant, and time-bound (SMART) goals, individuals can create a roadmap for their personal growth journey and reach their full potential.

Positive Self-Talk: Positive self-talk is a positive habit that can improve self-esteem and reduce stress. By replacing negative self-talk with positive affirmations, individuals can improve their mental well-being and increase their self-confidence.

Gratitude: Practicing gratitude is a positive habit that can increase happiness and reduce stress. By focusing on the positive aspects of life, individuals can develop a more optimistic outlook and reach their potential with a positive mind set.

Examples of Negative Habits:

There are also negative habits that individuals should avoid to reach their potential. Some examples include:

Procrastination: Procrastination is a negative habit that can lead to missed opportunities, increased stress, and decreased productivity. By delaying tasks, individuals can undermine their potential and limit their success.

Negative Self-Talk: Negative self-talk is a negative habit that can reduce self-esteem and increase stress. By criticizing themselves, individuals can undermine their potential and limit their success.

Poor Time Management: Poor time management is a negative habit that can lead to missed deadlines, increased stress, and decreased productivity. By failing to manage their time effectively, individuals can limit their potential and hinder their success.

Unhealthy Eating: Unhealthy eating is a negative habit that can lead to poor physical health, decreased energy levels, and reduced cognitive function. By neglecting their diet, individuals can limit their physical and mental potential and compromise their overall well-being.

Substance Abuse: Substance abuse is a negative habit that can lead to addiction, physical and mental health problems, and reduced potential. By relying on drugs or alcohol, individuals can limit their potential and negatively impact their personal and professional lives.

Breaking Negative Habits:

Breaking negative habits can be challenging, but it is an essential step towards personal growth. To break a negative habit, individuals should first identify the cue, routine, and reward associated with the behavior. Once they understand the habit loop, they can create a plan to replace the negative behavior with a positive one. For example, if the negative habit is procrastination, the individual should identify the cues that trigger the behavior (e.g., feeling overwhelmed, lack of motivation), and the routine that follows (e.g., delaying the task, distracting themselves). They can then replace the negative routine with a positive one (e.g., breaking the task into smaller, manageable steps, setting a deadline, rewarding themselves for progress).

Developing Positive Habits:

Developing positive habits requires intentional effort and practice. To develop a positive habit, individuals should start by identifying the behavior they want to adopt and the outcome they hope to achieve. They should then create a plan to make the behavior a regular part of their routine, using cues and rewards to reinforce the behavior. For example, if the positive habit is exercising regularly, the individual should identify the best time and place to exercise, and create a routine that includes warming up, stretching, and cooling down. They can then use cues, such as setting an alarm or leaving their workout clothes out, to remind themselves to exercise, and reward themselves for their efforts.

Exercise is a form of physical activity that involves repetitive movements, such as walking, running, cycling, or weightlifting. Regular exercise has many benefits for physical and mental health, including:

Improved cardiovascular health: Exercise can strengthen the heart and lungs, lower blood pressure, and reduce the risk of heart disease, stroke, and other cardiovascular conditions.

Weight management: Exercise can help individuals maintain a healthy weight or lose excess weight, which can improve overall health and reduce the risk of chronic diseases.

Increased strength and flexibility: Exercise can improve muscle strength, flexibility, and endurance, making it easier to perform daily tasks and participate in physical activities.

Reduced stress and anxiety: Exercise can release endorphins, which are natural mood-boosters that can reduce stress, anxiety, and depression.

Improved cognitive function: Exercise can enhance cognitive function, including memory, attention, and problem-solving skills.

Developing the habit of regular exercise can be challenging, but it is a positive habit that can promote personal growth. Here are some tips for developing the habit of regular exercise:

Set a goal: Identify a specific fitness goal, such as running a 5K, lifting a certain amount of weight, or improving flexibility. Having a clear goal can provide motivation and focus.

Find a form of exercise you enjoy: Exercise should be enjoyable, not a chore. Try different forms of exercise, such as hiking, swimming, or dancing, to find something you enjoy.

Create a routine: Set aside a specific time and place for exercise, such as a morning walk or an evening gym session. Consistency is key to forming a habit.

Start small: Begin with a manageable amount of exercise, such as a 10-minute walk or a few basic exercises. Gradually increase the intensity and duration over time.

Track progress: Keep track of your exercise routine and progress, such as by using a fitness app or journal. Celebrate milestones and progress to stay motivated.

Regular exercise is a positive habit that can promote physical and mental health and support personal growth. By setting goals, finding enjoyable forms of exercise, creating a routine, starting small, and tracking progress, individuals can develop the habit of regular exercise and reap its many benefits.

Conclusion:

Habits play a significant role in shaping individuals' behavior and personality. By developing positive habits and breaking negative ones, individuals can reach their potential and achieve their goals. Positive habits, such as exercise, reading, goal-setting, positive self-talk, and gratitude, can help individuals improve their physical and mental well-being, expand their knowledge, and develop a positive mind set. Negative habits, such as procrastination, negative self-talk, poor time management, unhealthy eating, and substance abuse, can limit individuals' potential and compromise their overall well-being. By understanding how habits work and creating intentional plans to develop positive habits and break negative ones, individuals can achieve personal growth and reach their full potential.

Key points to remember:

1. Developing good habits can help you achieve personal growth by providing structure and routine to your life, which can help you focus on your goals and stay motivated.

2. Habits can help you break down larger goals into smaller, more manageable tasks that can be accomplished on a daily basis, leading to a sense of progress and accomplishment over time.

3. Consistency is key to building lasting habits, and it's important to stay committed to your goals even when faced with obstacles or setbacks.

4. It's important to stay open to new experiences and opportunities for growth, and to be willing to step outside of your comfort zone in order to achieve your full potential.

5. Habits can also help you cultivate a growth mindset, which is characterized by a belief that your abilities and intelligence can be developed through hard work and dedication.

6. Self-reflection and mindfulness can help you identify areas where you can improve and develop new habits that support your personal growth.

7. It's important to set realistic goals and to celebrate your progress along the way,

as this can help you stay motivated and committed to your habits.

8. Building a supportive network of friends, family, or colleagues who share your goals and values can provide encouragement and accountability as you work to reach your potential.

9. Finally, remember that personal growth is a lifelong journey, and it's important to approach it with a sense of curiosity, openness, and willingness to learn and grow.

Chapter 13: Overcoming Procrastination: Strategies for Taking Action and Avoiding Distractions

Prashant had struggled with procrastination in the past. He often found himself putting off tasks until the last minute, which caused him stress and made it difficult for him to achieve his goals. He realized that he needed to develop strategies to overcome his tendency to procrastinate and stay focused on his priorities.

One of the first strategies that Prashant used to overcome procrastination was to break down his tasks into smaller, more manageable steps. By focusing on just one small step at a time, he was able to avoid feeling overwhelmed and stay motivated to keep working. For example, instead of trying to clean his entire house in one day, he would focus on cleaning one room at a time.

Another strategy that Prashant found helpful was to eliminate distractions. He realized that he was often wasting time on social media or other forms of entertainment when he should have been working on important tasks. So, he started using apps and software that would block access to distracting websites and limit his time on social media.

Prashant also found it helpful to set specific goals and deadlines for himself. By setting clear objectives and deadlines, he was able to stay motivated and avoid procrastination. He also made a point to celebrate his successes along the way, which helped him stay positive and motivated.

Another strategy that Prashant found helpful was to develop a habit of prioritizing his most important tasks first thing in the morning. He realized that he was often more productive in the morning and that by tackling his most important tasks first thing, he was able to start his day off on a positive note and avoid feeling overwhelmed later on.

Prashant also learned the importance of taking breaks and giving himself time to recharge. He realized that he was often more productive when he took regular breaks and made time for relaxation and self-care.

Prashant overcame his tendency to procrastinate by breaking down tasks into smaller steps, eliminating distractions, setting clear goals and deadlines, prioritizing his most important tasks, taking regular breaks, and practicing self-care. By developing these habits, he was able to stay focused on his goals and achieve success in both his personal and professional life.

Procrastination is a common problem that many people face. It's the tendency to delay or put off tasks that need to be completed, usually leading to increased stress and anxiety. However, there are strategies you can use to overcome procrastination and take action. Here are some strategies, along with examples, that you can use to avoid distractions and increase your productivity.

Set goals and make a plan:

Setting specific, measurable goals is the first step in overcoming procrastination. It's important to identify what needs to be accomplished and create a plan for achieving it. This can help break down large tasks into smaller, more manageable steps, making it easier to get started. For example, if your goal is to write a research paper, you might break it down into the following steps:

- Research sources: Spend 2 hours finding relevant sources for the paper.

- Create an outline: Spend 1 hour organizing your thoughts and creating an outline for the paper.

- Draft each section: Spend 2 hours writing the introduction, body, and conclusion sections of the paper.

By breaking down the task into smaller steps, you can see progress being made and feel a sense of accomplishment.

Prioritize your tasks:

Prioritizing tasks is key to avoiding procrastination. It's important to focus on completing the most important tasks first, rather than getting side tracked by less important tasks. One way to prioritize tasks is to use the Eisenhower Matrix, which categorizes tasks as follows:

- Urgent and important: These are tasks that require immediate attention and have a significant impact on your goals.

- Important but not urgent: These are tasks that are important for your goals, but do not require immediate attention.

- Urgent but not important: These are tasks that require immediate attention, but do not have a significant impact on your goals.

- Neither urgent nor important: These are tasks that can be postponed or delegated to others.

By prioritizing tasks using the Eisenhower Matrix, you can focus on the most important tasks and avoid getting side tracked by less important ones.

Use a timer:

Using a timer can help you stay focused on a task and avoid distractions. The Pomodoro technique is a popular method that involves setting a timer for a specific amount of time, such as 25 minutes, and working on a task for that entire time. After the timer goes off, take a short break and then start another timer for the next task. This can help you stay focused and avoid getting side tracked by distractions. For example, if you need to clean your house, you might set a timer for 25 minutes to clean the living room, and then take a five-minute break before setting another timer for 25 minutes to clean the kitchen.

Eliminate distractions:

Distractions can be a major obstacle to productivity. It's important to identify the things that distract you the most and find ways to eliminate or reduce them. Some common distractions include social media, email, phone calls, and people interrupting you while you work. To avoid these distractions, you might:

- Log out of your social media accounts during work hours.
- Use an app that limits your access to social media during certain times of the day.
- Put your phone on silent or leave it in another room while you work.
- Close your email inbox and only check it at certain times of the day.
- Set clear boundaries with co-workers or family members about when you are working and need uninterrupted time.

By eliminating distractions, you can stay focused on your tasks and be more product

Hold yourself accountable:

Holding yourself accountable is another effective strategy for overcoming procrastination. This can be done by sharing your goals and progress with someone else who can hold you accountable. This could be a friend, family member, or co-worker who has similar goals or can provide support and encouragement. You might also consider using a productivity app that tracks your progress and sends reminders. By holding yourself accountable, you can stay motivated and on track towards your goals.

Reward yourself:

Finally, it's important to reward yourself for making progress and achieving your goals. Rewards can help motivate you to keep going, especially when the task at hand is difficult or not enjoyable. The key is to choose rewards that are meaningful to you and that you can look forward to. For example, if you've completed a major project at work, you might reward yourself by taking a day off or treating yourself to a nice dinner. If you've been studying for a big exam, you might reward yourself by taking a weekend trip or buying a new book.

It's important to remember that rewards should be used in moderation and should not be a way to avoid work or distract yourself from your goals. Instead, use them as a way to celebrate your progress and stay motivated.

Overcoming procrastination requires a combination of strategies that focus on setting goals, prioritizing tasks, eliminating distractions, holding yourself accountable, and rewarding yourself. By using these strategies, you can break free from the cycle of procrastination and take action towards achieving your goals. It takes time and effort to develop these habits, but the benefits of increased productivity and reduced stress are well worth it.here's an example of how someone might use the strategies to overcome procrastination:

Let's say that Jack is a student who has been procrastinating on a major project for his history class. He has known about the project for weeks, but has been putting it off because he feels overwhelmed by the amount of research and writing that needs to be done. Here's how Jack might use the strategies to overcome his procrastination:

Jack decides to break down the project into smaller, more manageable tasks. He sets a goal of completing the research phase of the project within the next two days. He creates a plan for achieving this goal, which includes identifying the key research questions, finding relevant sources, and taking detailed notes.

Jack uses the Eisenhower Matrix to prioritize his tasks. He identifies the research phase of the project as urgent and important, and decides to focus on that first, rather than getting side tracked by less important tasks like checking his email or social media.

Jack decides to use the Pomodoro technique to stay focused and avoid distractions. He sets a timer for 25 minutes and works on his research for that entire time, without checking his phone or email. After the timer goes off, he takes a five-minute break to stretch and clear his mind before setting another timer for the next 25-minute work period.

Jack identifies social media as his biggest distraction, so he logs out of all his social media accounts and uses an app that limits his access to them during work hours. He also puts his phone on silent and only checks his email at certain times of the day.

Jack shares his goals and progress with a study partner who also has a major project to complete. They check in with each other daily to provide support and encouragement, and to hold each other accountable for making progress.

Once Jack completes the research phase of the project, he rewards himself with a movie night and a favorite snack. He sets another goal for the next phase of the project, and plans a larger reward for when the project is complete.

By using these strategies, Jack is able to overcome his procrastination and make significant progress on his project. He stays focused, motivated, and on track towards achieving his goal.

In conclusion, overcoming procrastination is possible by setting goals and making a plan, prioritizing your tasks, using a timer, eliminating distractions, holding yourself accountable, and rewarding yourself. By using these strategies, you can increase your productivity and reduce stress and anxiety.

Key points to remember:

- Procrastination is a common behavior that can be caused by various factors, including fear, perfectionism, lack of motivation, and distractions.

- Procrastination can have negative consequences, such as stress, anxiety, missed opportunities, and decreased productivity.

- To overcome procrastination, you need to identify the root causes of your procrastination and develop strategies to address them.

- Some effective strategies for overcoming procrastination include setting clear goals, breaking tasks into smaller, more manageable steps, creating a structured schedule, prioritizing tasks, eliminating distractions, and using positive self-talk.

- It's also important to practice self-compassion and forgive yourself for past procrastination.

- Finally, it's important to recognize that overcoming procrastination is an ongoing process, and it requires consistent effort and self-reflection.

Chapter 14: The Role of Environment in Habit Formation: How to Create a Space That Supports Positive Change

The environment plays a significant role in habit formation. Our physical surroundings can either help or hinder our efforts to develop good habits. When we create a space that supports positive change, we make it easier to develop new habits and stick to them over time.

Prashant recognized this and took steps to create a space that supported his positive changes. He began by decluttering his home and removing anything that didn't serve a purpose or bring him joy. This helped him clear his mind and reduce distractions, making it easier to focus on his goals.

He then organized his space in a way that supported his new habits. For example, he created a designated area for his yoga mat and meditation cushion, which helped him develop a regular yoga and meditation practice. He also stocked his kitchen with healthy snacks, making it easier to resist the temptation of junk food.

Prashant also added visual reminders of his goals to his environment. He put up motivational posters and images of his ideal self to keep him focused on his vision of a healthier and happier life.

Finally, he enlisted the support of his friends and family to hold him accountable and keep him motivated. He shared his progress with them and asked for their encouragement and feedback.

By creating a space that supported his positive changes, Prashant was able to make lasting progress towards his goals. He developed healthy habits and overcame the obstacles that had held him back in the past. By recognizing the role of environment in habit formation and taking steps to create a supportive space, he was able to achieve success and transform his life.

The environment in which we live, work, and spend our time can have a significant impact on our habits and behaviors. The space around us can either support or hinder our efforts to form new habits and make positive changes in our lives. In this response, we will explore the role of environment in habit formation and provide some tips for creating a space that supports positive change.

1. Minimize distractions:

One of the biggest challenges to forming new habits is the presence of distractions that can pull us away from our goals. To create an environment that supports positive change, it is important to minimize distractions as much as possible. This might mean turning off the TV or other devices, closing the door to your workspace, or finding a quiet spot to work.

> If you're trying to create a new habit of reading every day, you might create a designated reading space that's quiet and free from distractions like TV or other devices. This could be a cozy reading book in your bedroom or a comfortable chair in a quiet corner of your living room.

2.Set up your space for success:

Your physical surroundings can have a big impact on your ability to form new habits. If you're trying to create a new exercise routine, for example, it's important to have a space that's comfortable, well-lit, and equipped with the necessary tools or equipment. If you're trying to improve your diet, you might stock your kitchen with healthy foods and eliminate junk food or other unhealthy temptations.

> If you're trying to create a new habit of exercising regularly, you might invest in some basic exercise equipment like dumbbells or a yoga mat, and set up a dedicated workout space in your home. This could be a spare room or a corner of your living room where you can do your workouts without any interruptions.

3.Make it visually appealing:

Your environment can also impact your mood and motivation. A cluttered, dark, or uninviting space can make it difficult to feel inspired or energized. To create a space that supports positive change, try to make it visually appealing with art, plants, or other decor that brings you joy and helps you feel motivated.

> If you're trying to create a new habit of eating healthy, you might make your kitchen more visually appealing by adding fresh fruits and vegetables to your countertops or displaying healthy recipes on your fridge. You could also invest in some new cookware or kitchen

gadgets that make healthy cooking more fun and enjoyable.

Create a routine:

4. **Creating a routine** around your new habits can help you stay on track and make progress towards your goals. Try to establish a consistent time and place for your new habit. For example, if you're trying to meditate every day, you might create a designated meditation space and commit to meditating at the same time each day.

If you're trying to create a new habit of meditating every day, you might create a designated meditation space in your home that's comfortable and quiet. You could also establish a specific time each day when you'll meditate, such as right after you wake up in the morning or before you go to bed at night.

5.Surround yourself with positive influences:

Finally, the people around us can have a big impact on our habits and behaviors. To create an environment that supports positive change, try to surround yourself with people who are supportive of your goals and who can provide positive influence and accountability. You might join a group or community of people who share your interests or goals, or you might work with a coach or mentor who can provide guidance and support.

> If you're trying to create a new habit of running every day, you might join a local running club or find a running partner who can provide support and accountability. You could also follow social media accounts or blogs of people who inspire you with their running stories or tips.

In summary, the environment in which we live and work can have a big impact on our habits and behaviors. By creating a space that supports positive change, minimizing distractions, setting up for success, making it visually appealing, creating a routine, and surrounding ourselves with positive influences, we can increase our chances of successfully forming new habits and achieving our goals.

Key points to remember:

- Our physical surroundings can either help or hinder our efforts to develop good habits.

- Creating a space that supports positive change makes it easier to develop new habits and stick to them over time.

- Decluttering and organizing your environment can help reduce distractions and clear your mind.

- Designating specific areas for different activities can help you develop and maintain new habits.

- Stocking your environment with healthy options can help you resist the temptation of unhealthy choices.

- Adding visual reminders of your goals can help keep you focused and motivated.

- Enlisting the support of friends and family can provide accountability and motivation.

- Taking steps to create a supportive space can help you make lasting progress towards your goals and transform your life.

Chapter 15: Sustaining Good Habits: How to Maintain Progress and Avoid Relapse

Developing good habits is important, but sustaining them is equally challenging. Many people start out strong, but struggle to maintain their progress over time. Here are some ways Prashant sustained his good habits:

1. **Celebrated small wins:** Prashant celebrated every small win to keep himself motivated. He acknowledged and appreciated his progress, no matter how small it was.

2. **Tracked his progress:** Prashant kept track of his progress to stay motivated and hold himself accountable. He maintained a journal of his daily activities, which helped him see how far he had come and where he needed to improve.

3. **Remained flexible:** Prashant remained flexible with his routines and habits. He understood that life happens, and sometimes things don't go as planned. He didn't beat himself up if he missed a day or two of his habits, but rather got back on track as soon as he could.

4. **Cultivated mental resilience:** Prashant practiced techniques to overcome obstacles and setbacks. He didn't let failures or setbacks deter him from his goals but instead learned from them and adjusted his approach.

5. **Celebrated the benefits:** Prashant focused on the benefits of his good habits, such as increased energy and improved mood. He reminded himself of these benefits whenever he felt demotivated.

6. **Developed a support network:** Prashant built a support network of friends and family who encouraged and motivated him. He shared his progress with them, and they celebrated his wins together.

7. **Continued learning:** Prashant continued learning and seeking new ways to improve his habits. He read books, listened to podcasts, and attended workshops related to his goals.

By following these strategies, Prashant was able to sustain his good habits and avoid relapse. He understood that building good habits was a lifelong process and remained committed to his goals.

Once you've established a new habit and made progress towards your goals, it's important to maintain that progress and avoid relapse. Here are some tips for sustaining good habits and maintaining progress:

1. **Celebrate small wins:**

   It's important to acknowledge and celebrate the progress you've made, even if it's small. This can help to keep you motivated and engaged in the process. For example, if you're trying to establish a habit of running every day, you might celebrate each week that you stick to your schedule by treating yourself to a massage or a new pair of running shoes.

   Let's say you're trying to establish a habit of writing every day. You might celebrate each day that you write for at least 30 minutes by rewarding yourself with a cup of your favorite tea, listening to your favorite song, or taking a short walk outside. This can help you to stay motivated and engaged in the process, and to recognize the progress you're making.

2. Practice self-compassion:

When you experience setbacks or relapses, it's important to be kind to yourself and avoid negative self-talk. Recognize that setbacks are a natural part of the process and that you can learn from them and use them as an opportunity to improve. For example, if you miss a day of exercise, try not to beat yourself up about it. Instead, focus on the progress you've already made and recommit to your goal for the next day.

If you're trying to establish a habit of meditating every day, you might practice self-compassion by acknowledging that it's okay to miss a day or two, and that setbacks are a natural part of the process. Instead of beating yourself up about it, you might focus on the progress you've made and recommit to your goal for the next day.

2. Create accountability:

Creating accountability can be an effective way to maintain progress and avoid relapse. This can be done by enlisting the support of a friend, family member, or coach who can provide encouragement and hold you accountable. You might also consider joining a group or community of people who share your goals and can provide a sense of community and support.

If you're trying to establish a habit of going to the gym three times a week, you might create accountability by enlisting the support of a friend or family member who can provide encouragement and hold you accountable. You might also consider joining a gym class or personal training program where you'll be held accountable by a coach or group of peers.

4. Anticipate and plan for challenges:

It's important to anticipate and plan for challenges that might arise as you work to maintain your habit. For example, if you're trying to eat healthy, you might plan for situations like traveling or attending social events where healthy food options might be limited. By anticipating these challenges and planning ahead, you'll be better equipped to stick to your habit and avoid relapse.

If you're trying to establish a habit of eating healthy, you might anticipate and plan for challenges like traveling or attending social events where healthy food options might be limited. You might plan ahead by bringing healthy snacks or meals with you, or by doing some research to find healthy restaurants in the area

5. Continuously adapt and adjust:

As you work to sustain your habit, it's important to be flexible and willing to adapt and adjust as needed. This might mean changing your routine, revising your goals, or trying new strategies. By being open to new ideas and willing to make adjustments, you can stay engaged in the process and avoid feeling stuck or stagnant.

If you're trying to establish a habit of reading every day, you might continuously adapt and adjust by trying different genres or authors, or by setting new goals for the number of books you want to read each month. By being open to new ideas and willing to make adjustments, you can stay engaged in the process and avoid feeling stuck or stagnant.

In summary, sustaining good habits and maintaining progress can be challenging, but it's possible with the right strategies and mind set. By celebrating small wins, practicing self-compassion, creating accountability, anticipating and planning for challenges, and continuously adapting and adjusting, you can stay motivated and make long-term progress towards your goals.

Key points to remember:

- Developing good habits is important, but sustaining them is equally challenging.

- Celebrating small wins can help you stay motivated and committed to your goals.

- Tracking your progress can help you hold yourself accountable and see how far you've come.

- Remaining flexible with your habits and routines can help you adjust to life's challenges.

- Cultivating mental resilience can help you overcome obstacles and setbacks.

- Focusing on the benefits of your good habits can help you stay motivated.

- Building a support network can provide encouragement and motivation.

- Continuing to learn and seek new ways to improve your habits can help you maintain progress and avoid relapse.

Epilogue

As we come to the end of this journey on the art of habit mastery, I hope that the insights and strategies shared in this book have helped you develop positive habits, break negative ones, and create lasting change in your life.

Remember that habit mastery is not a one-time achievement, but an ongoing process. As you continue on your journey, keep in mind that setbacks and obstacles are a natural part of the process, and that the key to success is to stay persistent and resilient.

I hope that the stories, examples, and case studies shared in this book have inspired and motivated you to continue on this path of personal growth and self-improvement. Always remember that the power to change your life lies within you, and that by mastering your habits, you can create a life that is fulfilling, productive, and joyful.

Finally, I want to thank you for joining me on this journey. I am grateful for the opportunity to share my insights and experiences with you, and I wish you all the best in your pursuit of habit mastery. May you continue to grow, learn, and thrive in all areas of your life.

www.ingramcontent.com/pod-product-compliance
Lightning Source LLC
LaVergne TN
LVHW010556160826
845677LV00013B/3148

* 9 7 9 8 8 8 9 7 5 7 2 7 6 *